GRUMPY OLD

MENOPAUSE

CAROL E WYER

Safkhet
Publishing

First published in 2013 by Safkhet Select, London, United Kingdom
Safkhet Select is an imprint of Safkhet Publishing
www.safkhetpublishing.com

Text Copyright 2013 by Carol E Wyer
Design Copyright 2013 Safkhet Publishing

Carol E Wyer asserts the moral right to be identified as the author of this work
under the Copyright, Designs and Patents Act 1988.

ISBN 978-1-908208-26-2

All characters and events in this publication,
other than those clearly in the public domain, are fictitious
and any resemblance to real persons, living or dead, is purely coincidental.

All rights reserved. No part of this publication may be reproduced,
stored in or introduced into a retrieval system, or transmitted, in any form or by any
means, including but not limited to electronic, mechanical, photocopying or recording,
without the prior written permission of the publisher.

Printed and bound by Lightning Source International

Typeset in Crimson, Ale and Wenches, and You Murderer BB with Adobe InDesign

Find out more about Carol on www.carolewyer.co.uk
and www.facing50withhumour.com
and meet her on Facebook at
www.facebook.com/pages/Carol-E-Wyer/221149241263847

Carol E Wyer	author
Kim Maya Sutton	managing editor and cover artist
Sally Neuhaus	cover designer
Walter Richardson	proofreader
William Banks Sutton	copy editor

 The colophon of Safkhet is a representation of the ancient Egyptian goddess of wisdom
and knowledge, who is credited with inventing writing.
Safkhet Publishing is named after her because the founders met in Egypt.

INTRODUCTION

Have you started to write post-it notes with your kids' names on them? Do you need to change your underwear after every sneeze? Guess it's time to read this book then. It'll help you get through "that" time in your life with a spring in your step and a smile on your face. (Yeah right!)

I hit puberty late in life. When I say late, I mean late. Every girl in my class had huge breasts, Bic disposable razors, and boyfriends, and giggled a lot about sex. I was behind the times and my body didn't transform until I was about seventeen.

Now, I am in my fifties and I am still a late developer. All my friends journeyed through the miserable menopause several years ago while I trailed behind.

At least I was able to amass a stack of information to help me transit this time with the minimum of woe and bad temper. I learned much from my friends and have discovered that you can get through the menopause without wanting to rip off people's heads or lying in bed with terrible cramps.

This guide will help you when your other half and your family don't seem to understand what is happening to you. It will ease your mind, when you are awake at night, wondering if you are the only woman in the universe to be swimming in a puddle of sweat with your heart palpitating. This little book will help you sail through a tricky part of a woman's life with ease and humour. It should prevent you from turning into Mrs Crabby or worse still, a demonic monster.

I would make sure you haven't got any sharp knives around the house though just in case I happen to be wrong.

Menopause is one of those life changes. How we handle it is up to us. Whether we choose to use hormone therapy replacement, whether we set up our own physical and mental regime through exercise, diet, or other means, or whether we decide to "go it alone" and just ride it out until it's hopefully over, we are entirely responsible for the daily attitude we carry throughout this time.

The menopause often occurs at a time in our lives when most, if not all, of our children are leaving or have left the nest. (For some, it unfortunately happens when their off-spring are going through puberty which can cause fireworks.) We may begin to feel needed less. Our purpose in life seems to have left, along with its dirty washing and noisy music. It is a time when we might begin to question what lies ahead.

Now that we have more time to ourselves we may begin to notice those indicators of age: facial wrinkles, the drooping turkey neck, and the triceps that are turning into the infamous "bingo wings". It's not a very appealing picture. However, we should not be concerned with the "old" woman who is staring at us in the mirror. We should concentrate on the "new" woman on the inside.

What can we do to get through this phase of our lives? Surprisingly there is much that we can do to stop blowing up at people and having a rough ride. We can take measures to look after ourselves and ensure we do not get too overwhelmed by what is happening to our bodies. However, the best medicine of all is laughter.

So, without further ado, sit back with a small glass of wine, a large box of chocolates and this book.

*

question: what can a husband do when his wife is going through menopause? answer: keep busy. if he's handy with tools, he can finish the basement. then when he's finished, he'll have a place to live.

*

things you should hide from a woman going through menopause: axes, arrows, anything sharp and pointed.

*

Anger, anxiety, aggression, annoyed ... the letter A is shaping up to be a great start to our journey through grumpy old menopause.

Let's start with the big A for anger, otherwise known as being affronted, annoyed, antagonized, bitter, chafed, choleric, convulsed, cross, displeased, enraged, exacerbated, exasperated, ferocious, fierce, fiery, fuming, furious, galled, hateful, heated, hot, huffy, ill-tempered, impassioned, incensed, indignant, inflamed, infuriated, irascible, irate, ireful, irritable, irritated, maddened, nettled, offended, outraged, piqued, provoked, raging, resentful, riled, sore, splenetic, storming, sulky, sullen, tumultuous, turbulent, uptight, vexed, wrathful. There, feel better?

You don't? This is the time to buy one of those large punch bags that boxers use and hang it outside, preferably in the garage. Whenever you feel like smacking something hard, walk out to the garage and have six rounds with the bag.

Better still, paint a large face on it of someone you want to hit, give the bag a name and let loose. (Warning—be careful you don't rip your shoulder muscles. So far, it's taken me five months of physiotherapy to fix mine, and I yelp and swear every time the physio tries to work on it!)

If, like me, you have been banned from attacking people with heavy or sharp objects every time you fly off the handle, then you can always rely on your crafty female ways. After all, there are other ways to release your inner anger.

husband to wife: "when I get mad at you,
you never fight back. how do you control
your anger?"
wife: "I clean the toilet bowl."
husband: "how does that help?"
wife: "I use your toothbrush."

*

After a gruelling morning during which our garden was decimated by builders who were looking for a fractured water pipe, and Mr Grumpy complained bitterly about his lot in life, I went out to grab a quiet few minutes in a local coffee house.

It was three in the afternoon, and as I opened the door, I noticed that only two tables were taken and they were occupied by elderly people drinking afternoon cocoa. I breathed a sigh of relief, ordered my green tea and skulked off to sit at a table in a corner, where I unfolded my newspaper and set about working out the Sudoko.

Almost immediately, the front door opened and four women, plus pushchairs, barrelled in. They ordered drinks and extracted babies from the pushchairs. They then set about chatting at volume, oblivious to everyone else. Babies gurgled and squealed. One young child, released from his harness, squirmed out of his chair faster than a heat-seeking missile and ran up and down the cafe screaming, "Eeeh!"

You know how cats recognise that you are allergic to them, and come and sit on your knee making you sneeze? I think the same applies to irritating children who have an inner ability to realise that the miserable old boot in the corner does not want to be bothered. The child got visual, locked onto me and propelled himself with force into my chair leg.

The little darling then insisted on standing next to my chair staring at me while picking his nose.

"Go away," I growled. He decided at that point that I was even more interesting, grabbed the vacant chair next to me and climbed up.

"Clear off. Go back to your mother."

He sat kicking my chair with podgy legs and staring at me with a goofy smile plastered on his face.

Since I became a grumpy old woman I have decided that I don't like children. It's illogical, but that's part and parcel of the menopause. Well, it is for me. I don't mind children if they are kept quietly out of the way, or are behaving, but when they disrupt my day, or get into my personal space I turn into a hideous fiend.

My growls didn't work. I turned around to get the attention of the group of mothers who were yacking away.

"Excuse me. I have something here that belongs to you. I'd like to give it back."

A young woman dragged her attention away from her friends and with a mouth half-full of biscuit mumbled, "Come to Mummy Naafan."

"No!" screamed Nathan.

"I've got you a drink," she wheedled.

"No!" yelled Nathan, going red in the face, "No drink. No Mummy!"

"Please yourself, Naaf. I'll give it to Jessie."

The brat shouted, "No!" once more and continued to kick my chair with more ferocity. I snarled at him. He kicked more furiously. The woman went back to her conversation with little more than a shrug of her shoulders. She clearly thought he was safe with me and had decided to leave him to wander back when he felt like it. I had suddenly become an unpaid child-minder. A switch flipped in my head. I saw red.

Fortunately, some tiny voice managed to shout out before I lifted "Naafan" from the chair, hung him upside down by his foot, and hurled him into the toilet opposite my table.

I did what I needed to do, then stomped past the women, who were still talking, oblivious to everything, and left the coffee shop. No, I didn't harm him. I merely painted his face in lipstick and covered him in makeup from my bag so he resembled a small demon, and left him at my table stuffing his face with a large chocolate muffin. I also left a sign on the table which said, "Be grateful I didn't kidnap him. Pay more attention in future, there are some right weirdoes about!"

The menopause can make us do mad things but we can use it to our advantage too. Having spent several decades being generally chirpy and happy-go-lucky, losing "my rag" had led to some positive results in recent years. When I snarl, my hubby runs about and prepares dinner for me or pours me a glass of wine. (Very wise move on his part.) Frighten your own unruly kids or husbands by standing in the kitchen holding a knife and staring into space like Jack Nicholson in *The Shining* and they'll soon ask if everything is okay and help with the cooking.

*

SIGNS YOU MIGHT BE EXPERIENCING MENOPAUSE:
YOUR HUSBAND JOKES that instead of buying a wood stove, he is using you to heat the family room this winter. Rather than just saying you are not amused, you shoot him.

Q: how many menopausal women does it take to change a light bulb?
A: one! only one. and do you know why? because no one else in this house knows *how* to change a light bulb! they don't even know that the bulb is *burned* out. they would sit in the dark for *three whole days* before they figured it out. and once they figured it out, they wouldn't be able to find the light bulbs despite the fact that they've been in the same cupboard for the past seventeen years!

but if they did, *by some miracle of god*, actually find them two days later, the chair they dragged to stand on, to change the *stupid* light bulb, would still be in the *same spot* and underneath it would be the wrapper the stupid light bulbs came in because no one ever carries out the rubbish! it's a wonder we haven't all suffocated from

the piles of rubbish that are a foot deep throughout the entirehouse! it would take an army to clean this house! I'm sorry ... what was the question?

*

Let's move away from anger and all those negative emotions that wash over you to some of the wonderful delights that you might experience as your body changes.

Remember when you were a teenager and all the boys in your class used Clearasil to get rid of their spots, but you didn't need to because you just bloomed and had peachy skin? It could be your turn to need Clearasil. While the rest of your body gets older, your skin decides to go through a late stage of puberty, and you may develop **acne**.

Fiery spots will appear for no good reason and of course, they will appear on days when you really don't want them to, like your child's wedding day, and for good measure, they will appear in the most prominent place possible—usually, near or on your nose. Even with extra strong foundation, layered on with a trowel, you will see the crimson spot shining. If you get a hot flush it will even glow. Sounds like Rudolph the Reindeer could have been female.

As you may know at the heart of acne lies the pimple. It's a plug of fat, skin debris, and keratin stuck in a hair duct. When it's open, it's called a blackhead. When it's closed over, it's referred to as a whitehead. Whiteheads often cause the walls of the duct to rupture. This in turn leads to redness, infection and acne.

It is best to wash gently twice a day than to scrub away at the spot vigorously, every morning. Please avoid squeezing it, as tempting as that may be. You could spread it. (Yes, I did!)

It will calm down. Acne isn't caused by poor hygiene. In this case it is most likely caused by your hormones. (They are to blame for so much.)

If you need to go out and don't want everyone to see your spot, then wear a ski mask or wrap a scarf tightly around your face. This method works well during cold weather but, of course, if it is summer, you'll look a total idiot. You could always invest in some leatherette trousers and a motor bike helmet, then you'll look like a cool cougar, and no one will realise that you are hiding a prize zit. (Might look a bit daft if you get into your Yaris still wearing the helmet.)

*

q: why did the police stop the greasy
teenager?
a: it was just a spot check.

*

To help cope with aforementioned symptoms, you could take up a demanding exercise class which will allow you to release your inner energy. That way, even if you get angry or annoyed, you will be too exhausted to do anything about it. Or you could seek out **alternative medicine** and **alternative therapies**.

I am not a doctor so you must take appropriate advice before deciding on whether you should follow the alternative path. I had rather hoped to stay on the pill until I was fifty, then hop onto HRT for the rest of my days, but my body didn't fancy that, so I took the natural route. I didn't bother with anything. Can't get more natural than that.

For those of you who would like to try alternative treatments, a health food shop has trained staff who will help you choose a product like Burt's Bees for your acne, along with other natural menopause treatments. They may direct you to Kava Kava, St. John's Wort, or Goat's Weed, also known as Hypericum Perforatum for anxiety. I'd just like to say here that even though St. John's Wort is a widely used supplement for menopause and in treating depression, there are specific things to avoid while taking it, such as alcohol, cheese, and any foods containing Tyramine. Additionally, if the woman is on any type of antidepressant, St. John's Wort should not be taken.

Quite honestly, anything that means I have to cut down on my daily glass of wine gets left well alone, so my own efforts consist of little more than drinking soya[1] milk, taking the occasional evening primrose oil tablet, and making sure I get plenty of exercise.

1   Note: Japanese women have fewer menopausal symptoms than any other nationality. That is put down to their diet which is high in omega essential oils and soya.

There is a vast range of alternatives to HRT so acquaint yourself with the possibilities.

There are a range of activities I can suggest beginning with the letter A that might help you transit the menopause and take your mind off the annoying symptoms: **aerobics, archery, art, antique collecting,** and **arm-wrestling** to mention but a few.

Become wackier and breed **alpacas.** These hairy goat-like creatures are wonderful mothers. When they are happy they hum to their offspring and each other. Who wouldn't want a humming alpaca? I watched a documentary set in France (*Little England,* ITV3), in which a retired couple had started up an alpaca farm. It had transformed the pair of them and made them appreciate life so much more. (I highly suspect moving to France played a part too.)

Another way to help stay calm is to use some relaxing **aromatherapy** oils. Aromatherapy involves using plants and essential oils for relaxation, spiritual health and psychological health. Could be just what we stressed-out hormonal women need.

You can either inhale essential oils or apply them to the skin. You can even put small droplets into a bath. Never put essential oils onto the skin undiluted. I got a wonderful angry rash through dropping lavender oil onto my wrist. It itched for weeks. Be mindful too of the fact that anything you apply to the skin has a real chance of being absorbed into the blood stream, so only apply small amounts and read all instructions before you use them. (I wish I had!)

Breathe in … and…breathe out! Hope you are beginning to feel appeased by my words. We'll leave the letter A and move along while we are beginning to feel slightly amused and more relaxed.

B

things you should hide from a woman
going through menopause: bombs,
bazookas, blowguns, blunt instruments,
and firearms made by browning, beretta,
barrett and bersa.

*

Brittle bones, breast pain, bloating, and **body odour**! Looking at this list of menopausal symptoms, there doesn't seem to be much to look forward to. Don't despair. It isn't too bleak.

*

signs you might be experiencing
menopause:
you take a sudden interest in
"wrestlemania".

*

Cheers! I was really pleased to discover that **beer** can alleviate some menopausal symptoms. It's true. Czech scientific research has unearthed some fascinating facts.

It has been suspected for some time that hops can have an effect on the hormonal system. Before the advent of machine pickers, women and girls picked the plants at harvest. This would often take about three weeks. It was observed that amongst the young girls picking hops that their menstrual periods would come on early. Later this was validated scientifically. It transpires that hops contain very high levels of phytoestrogens—between 30,000 IU (international unit) to 300,000 IU per 100 grams. The levels are at their highest when the plant is fresh.

Beer contains phytoestrogens found in hops. Phytoestrogens work by binding to oestrogen receptors and thus provide a mild oestrogenic effect on the body. Obviously, they are not as strong as regular oestrogen, but as the oestrogen levels decline in menopausal women this boost can have a balancing effect on the body.

Herbalists use hops for their mild sedative effects. Not only are hops good for sleeping problems, they are beneficial to people with nervous gastrointestinal and stomach problems too.

Oh yes, I think I warned you to keep off too much alcohol in chapter one, didn't I? Don't worry, those clever Czech people have also brought out an alcohol-free version that has a similar effect. So next time you are out shopping, don't forget to buy yourself a six-pack. Na zdraví!

*

SIGNS you may be experiencing the menopause: you need the Jaws of Life to help you out of your car after returning home from an Italian Restaurant.

*

If you have a problem with a bloated belly thanks to your irritating hormones, then avoid eating too many gassy foods at one meal. Foods like cabbage, broccoli, cauliflower, onions, beans, Brussels sprouts, corn, oats, potatoes, apples, pears, peaches, milk, soft cheese, and fluffy wheat are difficult to digest. Chew your food properly too because digestion begins in the mouth. I expect that you have read this all before and follow the necessary advice. If you still have a bloated belly then take up **belly dancing**.

What an amazing hobby for a woman. It accentuates all your curves, especially that rounded belly, and can help you discover your inner goddess. (I read that in a magazine once. My inner goddess is more of a Medusa at the moment.) I admit that I have had a go at this. I attended several classes, and to be fair, you do actually begin to feel much more feminine once you grasp the idea. (And stop guffawing.) You can convince yourself that you are enchanting and captivating by the end of a session or two. The women who attend are encouraging and there is a grace to the dance. By the end of my sessions, I was ready to be sensual and provocative and entertain my man.

Give a local centre a call and watch a performance. You'll be intrigued. Have a go yourself. I don't suggest you try and captivate your man while he is watching football though. Somehow, you wobbling your stomach at him while waving a dishcloth about and batting eyelids takes second place when Arsenal are playing Manchester United.

What about taking up something else that'll make you feel sexy, wanton and desirable? **Burlesque** is all about the slow tease. People love burlesque today because it incorporates all the old-school glamour, and satire, and highlights the female form—it's something that many women can actually see themselves doing.

Burlesque takes its name from the Italian word *burla,* meaning joke. so I was naturally drawn to it. So far I haven't managed to perform anywhere other than my bedroom in front of the mirror but I might venture out one of these days.

How much cardio can one get from shimmying your shoulders and wiggling your hips? Quite a bit, it seems. You'll soon be strutting, sashaying, and sweating with a gusto that would have made Cher proud.

Still not convinced? Sample a **Bollywood dance** class. All the way from Bombay to Britain there are classes springing up everywhere. They have become very popular for events, workshops and school parties. Even hen parties are booking classes. Buy a Bindi, a sari, and some bling, then let out that inner Bollywood star. There will be no time to worry about brittle bones once you get on the dance floor.

If that is all too tame for you and you want to blast that bloated belly away by taking up an extreme activity, you could have a go at **bungee jumping**. It's guaranteed to provide a lot of excitement and get your heart racing. I'm sure as you speed to the ground, your stomach will look flatter as it drags behind you.

It isn't looking so bleak, is it? As for alternatives to conventional medicine that begin with the letter B, I ought to mention **black cohosh** here. Black cohosh, a member of the buttercup family, is a perennial plant that is native to North America. Other common names for it include black snakeroot, bugbane, bugwort, rattleroot, rattletop, rattleweed, and macrotys. Insects avoid it, which accounts for some of these common names. It is therefore peculiar that a plant with such a variety of horrible names can supposedly help women during menopause. Some believe that it can alleviate hot flushes and other menopausal symptoms, but studies[2] reveal conflicting data on that subject. In short, the jury is still out on it, and while some say it is beneficial there have been others who suggest that black cohosh carries risks of headaches, dizziness, gastrointestinal disturbances and possibly liver toxicity.

If you are considering taking black cohosh then get professional advice before doing so.

Let's move on to hobbies or activities that might help you through the menopause. I had to mention this next one because it's what has kept me sane for three years: **blogging**. It couldn't be easier to set up a blog. Google "Wordpress" or "Blogger" and get started. There are instructions on the internet. Millions, and I mean millions, of women of all ages, blog regularly. You will find oodles of blogs about the menopause alone. These can be sassy, witty or just informative. Set up your own or work with a friend and write one together.

Don't fancy writing a blog? Read some of those that are out there in cyber world instead and comment on posts. There are a huge number to discover including: menopausetheblog. com, menopausegoddessblog.com, menopausemaniac.com, theperimenopauseblog.com, flashfree.me, and menopausalmonster. blogspost.com among many others.

*

a bloG is like a therapist. it's the first place you go when you want to moan endlessly about your life.

*

Join Facebook and sign up for one of the menopausal groups where members share worries and experiences. I was surprised at how many groups there are. Hang out with others at Menopause

2   http://ods.od.nih.gov/factsheets/BlackCohosh-HealthProfessional/

Sucks, Menopausechatter.com, Menopause Matters or Menopause Fitness. You need never be alone and suffer in silence again.

Should you enjoy reading, join or start a **book club**. Get together with a group of like-minded people and discuss the latest best-seller or something more appropriate like *How Not to Murder Your Grumpy* by Carol E Wyer.

Not adventurous enough for you? Then why not do the same as Lucy Valantine from the UK who decided that she needed to change her life and purchased a Harley Davidson. She spent the following five weeks riding through France and Spain, before embarking on a new life in Costa Rica as a teacher. She still rides her motor cycle. She now has a tattoo on her stomach of shells, seahorses and the words "Live Life". Oh yes, she's also found a new love interest too. Who'd have thought **bikes** could be so much fun?

For something different have a go at **bareback riding**. This can be challenging and exhilarating. Clearly, you would need proper instruction, but imagine the freedom of riding bareback over fields and dales, with the wind blowing in your hair. I can't vouch for it myself but I am given to believe that the very freedom of riding without a saddle challenges you as a rider but also allows you to be more in tune with your horse. Contrary to some beliefs, it does not require strength or bravery, just a good sense of balance. (And a large amount of padding for when you fall onto the ground.)

*

A POORLY-LOOKING HORSE LIMPS INTO A BAR
WITH A BANDAGE ROUND HIS HEAD. HE ORDERS A
GLASS OF CHAMPAGNE, A VINTAGE BRANDY AND
TWO PINTS OF GUINNESS.
HE DOWNS THE LOT AND SAYS TO THE BARMAN:
"I SHOULDN'T REALLY BE DRINKING THIS WITH
WHAT I'VE GOT."
"WHY, WHAT HAVE YOU GOT?"
"ABOUT 2 QUID AND A CARROT."

You might prefer my next option which does not require balance, merely a quick mind. It is very good for helping with your memory— bridge. (The game involving cards, not going out with a team of mates and constructing a flyover for the A38.)

If you haven't ever tried this game, here's your chance to take it up. Team up with three other fun-loving women, add a jug of Margaritas, spice up the game by putting on a little bet and you'll have a super time. (I'm sure I just described an episode of Desperate Housewives.)

Bridge is one of those games that requires good attention and memory so you'll be doing yourself a big favour if you take this up. Just don't ask me to explain the rules because I still don't understand them. Mind you, I think it was more difficult to play the game using that pack of "Old Maid" cards.

*

GIVING A MAN HIS PHYSICAL, THE DOCTOR NOTICED SEVERAL DARK, UGLY BRUISES ON HIS SHINS, SO HE ASKED, "DO YOU PLAY HOCKEY, FOOTBALL, OR SOME PHYSICAL SPORT?" "NO," HE ANSWERED. "I PLAY BRIDGE WITH MY WIFE."

*

I'll skip over any other suggestions such as **bowling** where you could release any aggression left over from losing at bridge by hurling a heavy bowling ball down an alley, and move swiftly on to the letter C.

C

thinGs you shoulδ hiδe fRom a woman GoinG thRouGh menopause; cutlass, cuδGel, club, cosh, colt (Gun), caRbine, cReδit caRδs.

*

Sorry, what letter are we on? I was thinking about...there I go again. Does your **concentration** slip from time to time? Try some of these concentration exercises:

- A candle flame—sitting in front of a candle and concentrating on nothing but the flame for five to ten minutes will enhance your powers of concentration considerably.
- Have a freezing cold shower—Brr! Think of all the things you are grateful for in life and your mind will be taken off the fact that your bits are almost frozen solid.
- Count from one hundred backwards down to one. This may sound simple enough, and it is, however, it takes a bit of concentration to do it.
- Recall a photograph—Study a photograph which is unfamiliar to you. Do this for five minutes and then try to recall as much as you can about the picture.
- Spell words backwards. Not much I need to say about this. Try it. It works. Don't try it on "supercalifragilisticexpialidocious". It just makes you cross.

Hope that helps with you know what ... where was I?

One minute you are going about your business in a perfectly normal way and the next minute you are sobbing for no apparent reason. I was browsing in a department store a while back. I intended to go through the bargain rail in the woman's department, so all was well in my little world. To get to the women's department you have to go through the children's department. As I walked through, determined to barge my way through the hundreds of women hell-bent on bagging a bargain, I noticed a yellow furry duck sitting on a shelf. It reminded me of Beatrix Potter's Jemima Puddleduck. I glanced at it, recalling that a very long time ago my husband and I had been browsing for gifts for our unborn child in a similar department store. We'd both fallen in love with a similar duck which played lullabies. We had seen the duck at the same time, squeezed hands and knew in an instant that we should buy it for our baby.

As I reminisced about that joyous moment, I suddenly felt hot tears splashing down my face. The tears flowed without restraint and became accompanied by large sobs. I had no control over either. I began to attract attention from other shoppers. That made matters worse, because ordinarily I travel under the mantle of invisibility that all people over fifty wear. Normally, I could march about the store stark naked, wearing a light shade on my head and no one would blink an eye, but today, a sobbing woman suddenly became highly visible. Another woman asked if I was all right. My shoulders shook and I managed between gulps of air and blobby tears to tell her that I was fine. I scurried away to the toilets where I sat and cried until, eventually, I could gather myself together. I tiptoed out past the shoppers in case any of them had seen me break down.

What can you do if that happens? I considered carrying a pack of onions around with me and say that the pungent aroma was making my eyes stream, but on the basis that you can't walk around with a string of onions around your neck all the time, then I suggest you occupy yourself enough so that you don't have any opportunity to cry.

The most obvious antidote is **comedy**. Ensure you have a good supply of pre-recorded or purchased comedy DVDs of all your favourite shows; whatever makes you laugh most. Our house is crammed full of old seventies comedy shows and even today they help. I try to make sure that we watch at least one thirty-minute comedy show each evening. If you really have run out of shows, search the internet and discover a few jokes a day.

I found out some time ago that the average healthy child laughs approximately four hundred times a day. The average healthy adult only laughs about fifteen times a day, and most people don't laugh at all. Well, that's pretty understandable given the state of the economy, social problems and, in our case, the fact we are getting older and have to deal with a rebellious body.

If you make an effort to try out a few jokes every day you will notice a huge benefit. I'll discuss the reasons why under the letter L later in the book, but for now, let's just try it out with today's comedy routine. Here are fifteen short jokes that I tried and tested on all my blog followers and people who follow me on Facebook and Twitter. "Feel Good Friday", my joke day on my blog, is visited more than any other post I put up, so there is clearly a need for humour/comedy.

*

why do seagulls live near the sea? because if they lived near the bay, they'd be called bagels.

what is small, red and whispers? a hoarse radish.

what's black and white and eats like a horse? a zebra.

what's green and sings? elvis parsley.

two silkworms had a race—it ended in a tie.

five out of every three people have trouble understanding fractions.

a computer once beat me at chess, but it was no match for me at kickboxing.

two antennas meet on a roof and fall in love. the wedding wasn't much but the reception was excellent.

a shipment of viagra was hijacked last week. police are looking for two hardened criminals.

did you hear about the actor who fell through the floor? it was just a stage he was going through!

why do cows lie down in the rain? to keep each udder dry.

patient: doctor, doctor i'm addicted to brake fluid. doctor: nonsense, man, you can stop any time.

phone answering machine message: " ... if you want to buy marijuana, press the hash key ... "

i saw this bloke chatting up a cheetah. i thought, "he's trying to pull a fast one".

two elephants walk off a cliff ... boom, boom!

i've trained my dog to bring me a glass of red wine. it's a bordeaux collie.

*

Okay, there were sixteen. I figured you could do with a bonus laugh.

Along the same lines as comedy, take up **clowning**. Hey, with the red acne and blotchy nose that I talked about in the first chapter, we are already set up to be clowns. Taking up clowning skills or circus skills is not as bizarre as you might initially think. Discover the clown within you by attending one of many courses worldwide. If you ever saw the film *Patch Adams*, you might recall how he used laughter to help sick patients. The film was based on reality and was about Hunter Doherty "Patch" Adams, physician, clown and author who founded the Gesundheit Institute in *1971*. After the film's release, one of my neighbours joined a team of like-minded people emulating Patch Adam's philosophy. They travelled to Russia and visited patients in hospitals. Like Patch Adams, they wore clown noses and tried to entertain the patients through humour. It was a "humbling yet rewarding experience" according to him.

Go the whole hog and buy a car that falls to bits when you drive it. (Imagine the fun as it pops and shudders every morning on your way to work, then the delight as the wheels tumble off it in the staff car park.) Don't forget to invest in a large checked or spotted baggy suit too. (It'll hide all that extra weight you've put on recently!) Get a bright orange wig (which will hide your thinning hair) and go and make someone laugh.

If that all sounds a tad extreme, at least sign up for, and participate in, Red Nose Day. Dressing up and wearing a large red nose can do wonders for your emotional health.

If the clowning about hasn't worked its magic then how about a little release for all that pent up emotion? What about taking up **combat sports**? These sports are not just for tough guys. They are for everyone and anyone. Many women participate in these sports, and there are even classes dedicated to only women. If you are going to cry, how about in frustration or because you have been slammed into the mat at a judo contest? At least you won't be whimpering for no good reason.

There are too many combat sports to make a listing for each, so here are a few possibilities: fist fighting, kickboxing, full contact karate and taekwondo, wrestling, beach wrestling, Brazilian jiu-jitsu, catch wrestling, freestyle wrestling, judo and sumo. (Ideal for those of us who really have piled on the pounds recently.)

There are also hybrid martial arts, combining striking and grappling elements such as: pankration, dambe combat sambo and sanshou. Or, you can use weapons and fight. Good thing you can't see my face at this point because I am grinning rather insanely.

This will help relieve any aggression remaining from the first chapter. Also try fencing, kendo (Japanese fencing), or heavy combat sportive stick fighting using a quarterstaff, singlestick, bâton français, or a Filipino stick.

I hope you consider taking at least one of these up. To get you pumped and motivated, why not reflect on what the first rule of fight club is?

Aerobic activity that makes use of your large muscle groups while keeping up your heart rate is a very good thing. Fortunately, your options for **cardio** are limitless: walking, jogging, biking, and swimming all count. Beginners should start with ten minutes of light activity, slowly boosting exercise intensity as it becomes easier.

Another suggestion that will ensure you don't have time to dwell on things that might make you cry is **climbing**. You could have a climbing wall constructed in your back garden but I was thinking bigger than that. Get yourself on one of those climbing tours that goes up mountains or volcanoes. I can assure you when you make it to the top of a mountain, and once you stare out into the distance at the views you will cry, not from pesky hormones but little tears of joy and pride. If you are going to cry, at least have something worthwhile to cry about.

Sure, physical activity is essential, but don't forget to exercise your **creativity**. This is an optimal time to indulge in an artistic outlet. Take an art class or even join a knitting group to engage in a creative new activity that will promote a sense of achievement and satisfaction, and help take your mind off of annoying symptoms.

I appreciate not everyone is fit enough to go mountain climbing so a simpler solution is to compile music collections to suit your mood. If you are having a low day and want to eat **chocolate**, watch sad films or shut yourself away in your bedroom and sob into your pillow, then make sure you have uplifting music ready on your iPhone or sound system. Purchase some "feel good" **CDs** in preparation for those down days. A few "pump it up" songs or good old seventies tracks will soon sort you out. I bet you didn't think that you could remember all the lyrics to *"Remember you're a Womble"* or *"Ernie, the Fastest Milkman in the West"*.

I hope you are feeling more cheerful at this point in the book. You ought to be humming along to *"Always Look On the Bright Side of Life"* and getting ready to face the day or evening ahead.

D

things you should hide from a woman going
through menopause: daggers, dynamite,
darts.

*

For thousands of years, the Chinese, Japanese, and Koreans have harvested the yellowish-brown, thick-branched **dong quai** roots for spice, tonics and medicine. The plant is harvest-ready in three years, when its root is at the apex of vigour and stamina, then it is harvested and formulated into tablets, powders, dried root slices, dried leaf, raw root, liquid, extract, tinctures, teas, ointments, and creams. The roots are believed to have different qualities—the head of the root has anticoagulant activity, the main part of the root is a tonic, and the end of the root eliminates blood stagnation.

It is considered to be the "female ginseng" because of its balancing effect on the female hormonal system. However, studies have not found dong quai to have hormone-like effects. I haven't tried it, but on the basis that I don't often get to type the words dong quai, I thought I'd add it here. Again, I would counsel seeking advice from medical professionals before charging into your health store and demanding it.

Depression, dizziness, diet, dread, doom, and **difficulty concentrating** are some of the dreaded Ds that you might experience as you go through the menopause.

*

basil fawlty: manuel ... my wife informs me
that you're ... depressed. let me tell you
something. depression is a very bad thing.
it's like a virus. if you don't stamp on it,
it spreads throughout the mind, and then

One day you wake up in the morning and you ... you can't face life anymore!
Sybil Fawlty; and then you open a hotel.[3]

*

I understand that depression is a very serious subject but the antidote is laughter. Laughter can help lift your mood. Humour therapy helps you to find ways to make yourself (or others) smile and laugh more.

I am a huge fan of laughter and more will be said about this in a later chapter, so without further ado let's see if these doctor jokes help lift your mood, and make you laugh.

*

Patient: "Doctor, doctor, I can't stop stealing things."
Doctor: "Take these pills for a week; if that doesn't work I'll have a colour TV."

Patient: "Doctor, doctor. I think I'm a bridge!"
Doctor: "What's come over you?"
Patient: "Oh, two cars, a large truck and a bus."

Patient: "Doctor doctor. What can I do? Everyone thinks I'm a liar!"
Doctor: "I find that very hard to believe."

Patient: "Doctor, doctor. I feel like a pack of cards."
Doctor: "I'll deal with you later."

Patient: "Doctor, doctor. I think I'm invisible."
Doctor: "Next please!"

---

patient: "doctor, doctor. i think i'm a bell."
doctor: "take these and if it doesn't help, give me a ring."

patient: "doctor, doctor. i think i'm a cat."
doctor: "how long has this been going on?"
patient: "oh, since i was a kitten, i guess."

patient: "doctor, doctor. can you give me something to make me better?"
doctor: "take 2 teaspoons of this after every meal."
patient: "but doctor, i've only got one teaspoon."

*

This is the chapter where I set aside my giant bag of wine gums and talk to you about **diet**. There is no getting away from the fact that at our age, we should all take extra care with our diet. It will make an enormous difference to how we feel or perceive ourselves if we take the trouble to eat properly. I'm aware of what I should eat, and I'm equally aware of what I shouldn't eat, but when a bumper pack of Chunky Kit Kats are in my cupboard, it requires more willpower than I have to not chomp on them.

*

a woman went to the doctors. he realised that all her problems were because she was terribly overweight, so he put her on a strict diet. he said to her, "i want you to eat regularly for two days, then skip a day. repeat this procedure for two weeks. the next time i see you, you should have lost at least five pounds."

when she returned two weeks later, she shocked the doctor by having lost nearly sixty pounds. "why, that's incredible!" the doctor said, "did you follow my instructions?" she nodded. "i'll tell you though, i thought i was going to drop dead on the third day." "from the hunger, you mean?" asked the doctor. "no, from all the wretched skipping."

how to be twenty per cent lighter (instantly):
introducing: l i t e! the new, light "weigh" to spell "light!" with twenty per cent fewer letters!

*

Having consumed over half the aforementioned wine gums, I am going to move on to **dizziness**. The first time I became dizzy and fell over was due to a night out and drinking far too many vodka shots. Today, sadly, it is for more sober reasons. Like many women, I often stand up and feel dizzy. In fact, I can feel dizzy when I am lying in bed. How bizarre is that? Dizziness during menopause is caused by, yes, you've guessed it, those hormone levels again.

Lifestyle changes and self-care are often the first steps in treating dizziness associated with menopause. Eating healthily, getting enough fluids, and exercising regularly can greatly help to reduce episodes of dizziness.

Women, like me, who get dizzy when they stand up, should take precautions to avoid getting up too quickly or making sudden postural changes. I often get my hubby to do the washing up by saying, "I've just sat down, and you realise what will happen if I stand up again. Besides, I'll drop the plates."

How should we distract ourselves from the above symptoms? Certainly we shouldn't drink alcohol since that's supposed to make symptoms worse. I have a better idea that is much healthier. What about drums?

"my bloody neighbour banged on my front door at 2.30 this morning. thank god I was still up playing the drums."

jo brand

*

There is nothing dumb about this suggestion. Not many people knew that Elizabeth McGovern—the fifty-one-year-old actress best known as Lady Cora in the popular television drama *Downton Abbey*—had a secret life as rock star until she appeared at the Isle of Wight Festival with her band, *Sadie and the Hotheads*.

Elizabeth began by taking guitar lessons then found herself writing songs about her life as a middle-aged, happily married woman. Her alter-ego Sadie was soon born, and a new life as a singer began.

In a world where many men with balding pates and expanding waistlines are rediscovering the joys of thrashing guitars and pounding drums, why not be like Elizabeth? Set your drum kit up in the lounge and bash away to your heart's content. If you gain enough confidence, form a band with other women and then set off on tour. I leave it to you to think of what name you'd give yourselves. *Minnie Paws and the Hot Flushes* has already been grabbed by yours truly though. See you on the circuit!

If you would like to join a ready-made band, I noticed an advertisement for a female drummer on the website www. exploretalent.com. The advert read "Female Drummer Needed, Las Vegas, NV Music Drums Las Vegas ... P.S. I promise we're not creepy middle aged men." What are you waiting for?

Another delightful distraction to beat those blues is **dancing**. Yes, you can sign up to all sorts of classes and learn tango, ballroom, or jive, but even putting on a golden oldie CD (I always favour Abba's *Dancing Queen* or similar) and having a jig about to it in the living room will work wonders. Warning: if the couple from number 42 are walking their dog and happen to peer in and see you attempting to breakdance, you will raise eyebrows.

I hope you are feeling less dreary and drained having read this chapter and are enthusiastically anticipating the next section. Just got to remove my sparkly stilettos and I'll be with you.

E

things you should hide from a woman going
through menopause: explosives.

*

I am going to have to start this chapter with some words about
exercise. Though frequent workouts haven't been proven as a means
of reducing menopausal symptoms, they *can* ease the transition by
helping to relieve stress and enhance your overall quality of life.
Regular exercise is also an excellent way to stave off weight gain and
loss of muscle mass—two frequent side effects of menopause.

Most healthy women should aim for at least a hundred and fifty
minutes of moderate aerobic activity or seventy-five minutes of
vigorous aerobic activity a week.

Your cardio options are fairly extensive, as machines like the
elliptical or the Stairmaster count, too. If you don't want to pound
the streets on a cold morning, then hit the gym to get in your cardio
sessions. Studies show that as you enter menopause, your risks for
cardiovascular disease (CVD) increase significantly. Oestrogen
levels, which are thought to protect your heart, drop during
menopause.

Exercise shouldn't be all hard work. If treadmills or jogging aren't
your thing, consider dance classes. I mentioned this in previous
chapters, so I don't need to repeat myself here.

There, now we have got that over with, I can go back to my wine
gums and continue writing this chapter.

*

I have a new incentive to do sit-ups. I put
m&ms between my toes.

every time I hear the dirty word
'exercise', I wash my mouth out with
chocolate.

you know you're still in good shape if you
can touch your toes. using your boobs
doesn't count.

I have flabby thighs, but fortunately my
stomach covers them.

*

It is possible to experience **electric shock** sensations during menopause. These electric shocks can affect the head and/or the layers of tissue under the skin. This menopausal symptom may occur in isolation or it may precede a hot flush.

There is some evidence to suggest that sensations of electrical shocks are the result of changing hormone levels during menopause, which has a direct effect on the nervous and cardiovascular systems.

Again, changing your lifestyle and taking supplements might help. In order to support your nervous system you might want to take vitamin B complex, vitamin E, calcium, and/or potassium.

Many women swear that after taking one capsule of **evening primrose oil** every day for two weeks a month, and four capsules daily one week prior to monthly menstruation, they feel better.

Several studies support the menopause and evening primrose oil theory. The evening primrose is unlike a primrose. It is a biennial plant that often has woody stems, willow-shaped leaves that taste somewhat like pepper, and a strong root system. When the primrose unfolds at night, it reveals a lemon-coloured flower that has an amazing sweetness. However, by dawn the next day, the flower already starts to wilt and die, thus the name.

Evening primrose oil is made from the plant's seeds, which contain special oil comprised of gamma linolenic acid. Most menopausal women simply do not get an adequate supply of essential fatty acids. These fatty acids help by producing compounds similar to hormones that help maintain membrane function, cut down on swelling and inflammation, constrict blood vessels, control pain, support the body's natural immune response, prevent blood clots, and so on.

On a personal note, I found that taking a couple of evening

primrose oil capsules for a week whenever necessary instantly relieved discomfort and breast pain.

Here's another little tip for you. Place a spray bottle of **Evian** water in your fridge. It will help you cool down when you are having a hot flush. (I got that tip from a French woman.) If you really can't bear to spend all that money on water, seek out an empty bottle with a spray top and fill it with tap water. Alternatively, you could remove all the shelves and food and then sit in the fridge when you get hot.

Emotions have a habit of running away with us at this time of our lives. One minute we are happy, the next we are angry or just sobbing. As mentioned in an earlier chapter, try to eat sensibly, exercise, pamper yourself from time to time and before you bite someone's head off, try to take a very deep breath. You don't really want to lash out at the ones you love, do you?

*

trusting a menopausal woman to control her emotions is like trusting a tornado to mow your lawn.

F

things you should hide from a woman going through menopause: fork, firearm, flail, flamethrower.

*

Fatigue is another common problem associated with menopause, making the woman feel completely worn out, often for no apparent reason. For this, there is a Chinese drug called Gingseng, which can be found in supplement form or tea. This works very well but can cause slight breast tenderness.

Given that I sport eye bags blacker than a panda's, I am well-qualified to talk about fatigue. Some days I walk about like a complete zombie waiting to go to bed again. I find exercise and **fresh air** usually help. It will pass, and often it is best to tire your body out, even if you feel a little jaded.

*

q: as people age, do they sleep more soundly?
a: yes, but usually in the afternoon.

*

If the fatigue is making you feel low, then much like I suggested watching comedy to lighten your mood, I am going to mention here that you invest in a few **films** to help you through those "down" days. Here are a few of my personal choices guaranteed to lift your mood:

First Wives Club (1996)
Three ex-wives (played by Goldie Hawn, Bette Midler, and Diane Keaton) hatch a plan in this comical flick about getting mad and getting even.

The Full Monty (1997)

Not just because it's about men disrobing. Who could not chuckle at that scene in the benefits office?

Toy Story (1995)

This is not for children. It can't be. It's far too funny. Love those little aliens.

Up (2009)

My absolute all-time favourite. A cartoon can inspire you to get in touch with your inner child and remember the simple pleasures in life. *Up* is a multi-layered story about a grumpy old man who finds out that it's never too late to take a risk and have an adventure —or make a new friend. An overeager and earnest eight-year-old and Dug, a dopey but lovable talking dog, add to the humour in this beautifully written and animated story that will have you laughing through tears.

The Sound of Music (1965)

Listening to music has been shown to ease symptoms of depression, relieve stress, and calm the heart rate. Research shows that music with a slower beat is more relaxing than other kinds, which is why *The Sound of Music* scores highly with me. The classic songs performed by Julie Andrews as Maria, and the rest of the cast include *The Sound of Music*, *Edelweiss*, and *My Favourite Things*. These tunes —plus the Alpine scenery, the love story between the Captain and Maria, and the daring escape from the Nazis —are guaranteed to lift your spirits.

Grab a large bag of popcorn and enjoy!

Now you are relaxed, it is time for a sensible menopause fact: The menopause is a natural phenomenon, which occurs in all women when their finite number of ovarian follicles is depleted. As a result, oestrogen and progesterone hormone levels fall, and luteinising hormone (LH) and follicle stimulating hormone (**FSH**) increase in response. Menstruation becomes erratic and eventually stops and there are a number of secondary effects described as "menopausal symptoms". FSH levels vary markedly during the perimenopause.

FSH levels may be helpful in confirming the menopause in later stages.

*

what do you call a fish with no eyes? a fsh.

*

Last month, I decided to bite the bullet and check myself in the magnifying mirror. I tend to avoid looking at my face since Hubby bought me a ten times magnifying mirror. I hate using it because it accentuates all my wrinkles. Sometimes it's good to have poor eyesight. I like my fuzzy blurry world. Still, once a month, I muster up enough courage to check out my face and make sure all is okay. Anyway, the shock of what I discovered almost sent me screaming out of the house. My eyebrows had decided to sprout. That wouldn't have been too bad except the hairs weren't in the right place. One hair curled just above my eyelid, another in the middle of my forehead and the rest were scattered about my face. I even had hairs sprouting from my chin. I had developed **facial hair**! A trip to a professional was called for.

I hot-footed it down to the shopping centre where they have eyebrow bars every other shop. You can grab a seat in a jiffy, with no appointment, and a woman with beautifully groomed eyebrows will set about yours with a piece of dental floss and a steely determined look on her face. After much pain and gritting of teeth, you should walk away with arched smart eyebrows.

In reality, I looked at best surprised, and at worst, resembled an alien. One of my eyebrows had lost most of its follicles, while the other had kept hold of a few of them. I looked, well, *weird* best describes it. It transpired that my eyebrows had disappeared. The few that had been there had been groomed out of existence. My eyebrows had simply fallen out. Or quite possibly, they had relocated to my chin and over my lip.

The woman suggested I got my eyebrows dyed at some ridiculous cost. My wallet said buy an eyebrow pencil. I should have listened to her because trying to draw on eyebrows every day is a nightmare, especially if, like me, you have astigmatism and are short-sighted. By the time I get close enough to the mirror to see what I am doing, I have usually steamed it up with my breath.

The result is that I look like I am perpetually shocked by life. That sort of suits me. If I want to look perplexed, I draw them on the wrong way round so I look cross or puzzled all day. Some days, for fun, I pencil one really high so I look quizzical. There is endless fun to be had with an eyebrow pencil and time on your hands.

So, all that nonsense brings me onto the problem of hair or rather, facial hair. The wretched stuff grows where you don't expect it to: chins, cheeks, foreheads, and even your lips. There is only one saving grace: at least it doesn't come shooting out of your ears like on some men.

I have read about all sorts of remedies for hair growth but my mother warned me to leave well alone. According to her, that little hair you pull out of your chin today will turn into a beard in a month if you keep plucking it.

I've decided I'll live with it for the moment. I'll try and keep the stray hairs under control and if they get out of hand then I'll take drastic action.

*

ways to amuse yourself as you go through the menopause:
ask a saleswoman whether a particular shade of panties matches the colour of your beard.

*

If you are looking to connect to other women who are experiencing similar problems, sign up for **Facebook**. You may think it is the domain of the young and is full of pictures of cute cats (it is, but you will also be able to join groups where women post their anxieties and problems about the menopause). Check out Menopause sucks! Menopause chicks, Menopausal Mother, Menopause Chatter or Menopause Matters. There is something for everyone and a surprising number of people who are happy to share their experiences with you or offer advice.

*

when I was kid, my social network was called "outside".

*

I was browsing the internet, as I do, for helpful information, when I came across some ideas for **fierce and fabulous** women. No one could be fiercer than me at the moment, so after I'd snarled at the computer for a bit, I checked out some of the suggestions. If any of the following appeal, then you too could be fierce and fabulous at this important time of your life. Some of these might help you forget all about the menopause:

- Go skinny dipping! No matter what your age, be proud of your body and display it with joy. (Don't try this on a cold February morning in the UK.)
- Dye your hair. Crazier and brighter colours are especially encouraged. (Don't bother with bright purple if you have light brown hair like mine. It goes mucky orange and drab in a few days!)
- Take a trip or cruise to a far out land. Think of obscure places such as Antarctica. (It'll be nice and cool there which must help with those hot flushes.)
- Have a nude portrait of you painted. Display it in your home with pride. (If it looks anything like the one I had painted, it should give everyone who visits you something to laugh at.)
- Test drive an expensive car that you'll never be able to afford. Ferraris and Lamborghinis come highly recommended, as does an SLS Mercedes. (Try to ditch the salesman to get better enjoyment by taking off before he climbs in beside you.)
- Drive fast. If concerned about breaking the speed limit or the law, take a trip to the race track.

As much as I don't want to discuss this, I feel duty bound to mention **flatulence** here. Some women experience more gas than they used to at this time of their lives. It can be embarrassing; however, I have a simple and efficient solution. Buy a large dog and every time you get wind, blame the smell on the dog.

Fish are supposed to make you feel calmer but I don't really want to stare at a tank of guppies all day, so what about a spot of **fly-fishing**. It's a calming and quiet hobby. Records show that women have been fly-fishing for years. It is not just a hobby for men. You get to wear waders—and who doesn't look good in waders—in a tranquil location, peacefully communicating with nature.

It's a recognised fact that women are actually better at this sport than men and land the biggest fish. There is some theory that it is to do with pheromones, which attract fish, but most people agree it's because women are good at listening and taking advice. Fly-fishing is very good for your mental health.

*

a man came home to be greeted by his wife dressed in a very sexy nightie. "tie me up," she purred, "and you can do anything you want." so, he tied her up and went fishing.

*

F is also for **forgetful**. Yes, who hasn't gone to the fridge and forgotten why they are there? I'm at that point where I have to make notes so I don't forget to do stuff, and then forget where I have put the notes.

*

an elderly husband and wife visit their doctor when they begin forgetting little things. their doctor tells them that many people find it useful to write themselves little notes.

when they get home, the wife says, "dear, will you please go to the kitchen and get me a dish of ice cream? and maybe write that down so you won't forget?"
"nonsense," says the husband, "i can remember a dish of ice cream."
"well," says the wife, "i'd also like some strawberries and whipped cream on it."
"my memory's not all that bad," says the husband. "no problem—a dish of ice cream with strawberries and whipped cream. i don't need to write it down."
he goes into the kitchen; his wife hears pots and pans banging around. the husband finally emerges from the kitchen and presents his wife with a plate of bacon and eggs.
she looks at the plate and asks, "hey, where's the toast i asked for?"

q: why should menopausal women use valet parking?
a: the valet won't forget where he parked your car.

*

Guess that's about it for fun facts and frolics with the letter F. Uhm ... what was I talking about?

G

things you should hide from a woman going through menopause: guns, grenades.

*

G is for what **gift** to buy for a menopausal woman. Well, she really needs help at this stage of her life, so why not give her a present she can appreciate? I don't mean some t-shirt, hat or a key ring with *Warning! Hormonal. May lash out irrationally without provocation!* I, for one, am very likely to thump anyone who buys me one of those.

Here are some sound suggestions for Christmas or birthday presents that might be appreciated:

- *Coldfront* are cooling palm packs that come in their own ergonomically designed carrying case. A package with a re-cooling core and an absorbent cloth makes life a lot easier than shoving ice cubes down your bra.
- A desk fan. Make sure it isn't too noisy or she'll get hot and bothered by the whirring.
- A menopause gift hamper from health food stores, packed with natural foods, like dried mango and nuts that help stabilize mood and also help the body adjust to hormonal changes. Make sure you add lots of liquorice in mine.
- What about *The Feel Good Cooling Mattress Pad*? This mattress works by interacting with skin temperature, which for me ranges from simmering to boiling. Can also buy one of the sister products which works the same way.
- Wicking sheets, which draw the sweat away from the body. The alternative is to get your hubby to change sheets while you are taking your fourth cool shower of the night.
- A pearl necklace—some of you are raising your eyebrows at that comment and I don't mean real pearls, or the rude alternative either. These are cooling pearl necklaces or bracelets where the oversized pearls are filled with the same non-toxic cooling gel used in ice packs. They can be

frozen over and over again. They also come in a travel case that keeps it cool. Alternative—move fridge/freezer next to bed and sleep with its door open.

- Tickets for *Menopause the Musical,* which began in 2001, and has enjoyed a successful run in many countries. I couldn't find any shows in the UK, but there are still plenty in the USA. I'm sure a few nights away in the Big Apple watching a funny show would help lift your mood.
- Nightsweat night gowns. They don't look too sexy but that may be a good thing, after all, sex is not exactly on our minds while we swim about the bed at night. Haralee Weintraub, who writes about menopausal problems on her blog and website, offers a range of pyjamas, nightgowns, sheets and pillow cases that help you "Enjoy a Restful Night Sleep." Check out her website http://www.haralee.com/.
- Gag gifts—light hearted gifts—see comment above. Purchase these at your peril. You may think we'll be amused by and laugh at the darn t-shirt with "the seven dwarves of menopause" or the baseball cap with the words "next mood swing in six minutes" emblazoned on the front, but inside we will be fuming.
- Tweezers and a magnifying mirror. Ladies, hairs will soon appear in the most unexpected of places on your face. You'll need the mirror to see them and try not to faint when you first glance at your reflection, please. It is magnified, remember.
- Spa packages—a wonderful day or overnight stay at a spa where you can be pampered and enjoy massages. Stay out of the sauna though.
- A toy fire extinguisher. I had to include one joke present and this seemed the funniest to me.
- Finally, I came across *LadyCare* in my research. I can't tell you any more than what appears on the website. It is a small magnetic button that you wear under your underwear. The site claims that it can help you combat most of your symptoms and there are indeed testimonials from those women who agree with that statement. I'll

let you decide for yourselves by giving you this address: http://www.ladycareusa.com/. Maybe you could tell me if it is any good if someone buys you one.

If you can't afford to buy a gift then make this amusing and practical survival kit gift for someone going through menopause: Place M&M's into a jar or bag and add this message:

"To temporarily calm your craving for chocolate, eat the BROWN one. At the first sign of hot flashes eat the RED one. Eat the ORANGE one to minimize depression. The GREEN one calms your frustrations when you want to be left alone. If you feel a headache coming on, eat the YELLOW one. The BLUE one reduces bloating. If all symptoms occur at the same time, eat the WHOLE bag."

Ladies, you could also make your own gift. Try crafting a paper plate menopause lady. No kidding. This was suggested by Barbara Younger on her blog http://friendfortheride.wordpress.com/2012/02/28/around-the-year/.

I spent an entire morning making one. I really should have done something more productive; however, it cheered me up for a while and amused the family.

Root in your cupboards and unearth one of those paper plates with the fluted edges that aren't very good for serving food, because your sausage always falls off them. I'm sure you have some left over from the summer of 1992, which was probably the last time we had decent enough weather for barbecues in this country.

Draw a happy face on one side of the plate. Colour the face to represent you when you are feeling cheerful. Give yourself a nice toothy smile. Add hair too. Turn the plate over and draw a grumpy face. This is you on bad menopause days. Add spots and a deep frown. Thread a large ribbon through the top of your plate and hang it round your neck.

Paper Plate Menopause Lady will alert friends and family to your mood. Flip the plate around depending on how you feel. Barbara also suggests a poem to read out to your friends:

"If Menopause Lady sports a frown,
That means I'm feeling oh so down,
When Menopause Lady's mouth is up,
Life's as happy as a buttercup!"

It'll make you smile, if nothing else.

Moving away from gifts and onto hobbies beginning with the letter G that might help you during this time. Feeling old and tired, I came across one that I rather fancied—**graffiti**. It appealed to the young rebellious me buried deep inside this old body.

You don't need to lurk about under cover of darkness with a spray can of paint and write rude words on your neighbour's fence. (Or even ruder words on your hubby's shed. Warning: When you have got over your strop and wish you hadn't been so childish, paint doesn't come off with scrubbing. You'll have to repaint the shed before he gets up and sees it.) This doesn't have to be an illegal hobby, and I would encourage you not to do it illegally. It's possible to find areas where graffiti is permissible.

"Graffiti" comes from the Greek "to etch" and there have been signs of graffiti much older than even ancient Greek culture. Anthropology notes graffiti in lots of societies: cave men, ancient Egyptians, Native Americans and so on.

To get started, you're going to need gear, such as a mask for ventilation (especially if you are working indoors), spray paint, plywood and a black book of your graffiti drawings. Hide at home to begin with and warm up by spraying on large plywood boards.

It's also wise to learn about graffiti and graffiti subculture before even thinking about finding other graffiti artists or putting up a piece outside. There's a whole new lingo that surrounds this hobby and a definite hierarchy. It'll make you feel very hip/cool/trendy as you'll have to learn the meaning of "toys", "throw up", "tagging", "bombing", and "rack", among other things. It's an education, so get prepared for a real change. Move over, Banksy.

Should you not be barmy enough to take up a hobby like graffiti, you may want to join the thousands of women who enjoy **gardening**. This is an excellent hobby for getting fresh air, exercise, and relaxing among some of nature's glories. Rewarding and calming, it is ideal for those of us who need to get away from the hustle and bustle.

You could even grow a **menopause garden**. Oh yes, you can not only enjoy planting and growing, but you could benefit from the plants you are cultivating. You could also consider planting some of the plants mentioned below but make sure you take advice before preparing them and taking them:

- Yarrow has been in use since ancient times. It is most commonly used as a poultice to stop bleeding and heal wounds, but recently, it has come to light that yarrow is also effective as a remedy for bladder infections and shrinking fibroids and haemorrhoids. The plant also aids progesterone production which could cause acceleration of hot flushes and night sweats. Yarrow can be used in teas, tinctures or infusions.
- St. John's Wort has been used for centuries as an antidepressant and nerve tonic both in America and in Europe. St. John's Wort also relaxes muscle spasms, relieves aches and helps soothe dry, itchy skin. To use St. John's Wort, you should harvest the flowers when they are in full bloom. It can be used in teas, tinctures and massage oils.
- Stinging nettles (I'm good at growing these) have the highest chlorophyll content of any soil growing plant. They also provide nourishment for those areas of a woman's body that produce natural oestrogen, i.e., the adrenal glands, the kidneys and the lungs. Nettles contribute to healthy growth of hair follicles, which can help prevent thinning hair and hair loss as we grow older. Make sure you are protected by thick gloves and use scissors when you are ready to harvest your plants. Cut the tender tops of the nettle plant before they blossom. Steam the plants immediately. This will soften the needles and make them easier to handle. Stinging Nettles green tea is surprisingly tasty. It's also fun to give it to your husband to drink. Video his facial expressions as he realises it is not his usual cup of Earl Grey.

- Vitex or Chaste Tree is a slow, gentle plant remedy for regulating the menstrual cycle, and can relieve endometriosis, and fibroids, and supports hormone producing glands.

Alternatively, go out to the garden, sit on the bench with a cool drink and enjoy the serenity while watching your hubby do the weeding. It has the same calming affect as many of the above herbs.

*

new gardeners learn by trowel and error.

*

Another natural menopause treatment which begins with the letter G is a supplement called **Ginko Biloba**. This particular supplement has been around for thousands of years, helping women get past what is often referred to as a "foggy brain".

*

since i've been getting older, my memory is not as good as it used to be. also, my memory is not as good as it used to be.

*

I read last week that we women should all have a go at something outrageous; hence my mention of graffiti above. At this time of our lives we tend to be more reckless than we used to be so why not **gamble**? I don't recommend that you take it up full-time but just once, go to a casino and bet £100 on a single roulette spin or blackjack hand. Imagine the adrenaline rush if you won. Chances are you won't win and then you 'll have to explain to your husband why he is eating baked beans all week because you blew all the housekeeping money, but if you don't have a go …

*

q: why isn't gambling allowed in africa?
a: because of all the cheetahs.

*

At this time of our lives we might have to consider wearing **glasses**. At our age, our eyesight is likely to be failing. Do not despair. This is actually good news. Not only can you no longer see your wrinkles but glasses are very fashionable nowadays. Thank goodness for Harry Potter! It is very trendy to wear glasses, so make sure you get a few pairs of stylish glasses to match your outfits. I have an outrageous blue pair, luminous green and purple. (I admit I have terrible dress sense.) They are all infinitely better than the pair of National Health Owl glasses I was forced to wear as a child. Who would have thought having poor eyesight could make you glamorous?

*

q: where do 50+ year olds look for
fashionable glasses?
a: their foreheads.

things you should hide from a woman going through menopause: hand grenade, handgun, harpoon, hatchet, hunting knife.

*

"Is it just me or is it hot in here?"

My friend has a fan in her office, a small battery-operated one that she keeps in her handbag, three in the kitchen and one in the bedroom. I fancy one of those that Spanish dancers wave about. They are sometimes lacy and have pretty patterns or miniature paintings on them. I have always thought they looked exotic—ever since I saw one in Benidorm in 1977.

I had to abandon the idea of a fan dance when Mr Grumpy refused to be seen with me peering over my ludicrously large fan, batting my eyelids at everyone. I think the castanets were getting on his nerves too. I just wave my hands about in front of my face now trying to whir air about.

Yes, the dreaded **hot flushes** (flashes in the U.S.) can creep up on us at any time. I was in a shoe shop a few months ago. It was really hot in there, and as I waited for the young assistant to find the pair of shoes I fancied, I shrugged off my coat, my jacket and my scarf. The lady behind the counter saw me disrobing and laughed.

"At least you didn't do the same as me," she ventured, "I was out at dinner with friends and my husband last week and I suddenly felt a hot flush coming on. Of course, it was cold, being January, but I heated up like a furnace. I whipped off my jumper that I had put on. I wiped my face and thought that I'd got away with it hoping no one had noticed I had just had a hot flush. My friends were sitting open-mouthed and my husband was aghast. I'd pulled off my blouse along with the jumper and I was sitting there in just my bra!"

Here's an explanation of what actually causes a hot flush, so at least you understand why you burn up. I knew that "O" Level in Biology would come in useful one day.

The hot flush is an alteration in thermal stability, which is maintained by the hypothalamus, a brain region located above the pituitary gland on the brain's floor. The hypothalamus operates the body's temperature regulation system. Oestrogen levels manipulate some functions of the hypothalamus. During menopause, as the ovaries produce less oestrogen, the hypothalamus senses and responds to the lower oestrogen levels by rapidly changing body temperature. The result may be a hot flush.[4]

You might want to consider some of the following for hot flushes: phytoestrogens, Black cohosh, Siberian rhubarb, acupuncture, hormone replacement therapy, or anti-depressants (SNRIs such as Effexor and Pristiq).

Chat to a medical person or someone who is qualified before embarking on a course of any homeopathic or herbal remedies—at least one study[5] has found that a combination homeopathic remedy can be useful in the treatment of hot flushes. This study found no adverse side effects from the treatment.

*

I have found the cure for hot flushes, chocolate! Does it work? I don't know and as long as I have chocolate, I don't care.

*

If we are going to get heated we may as well have a good reason to break out into a sweat. Taking up the **hula hoop** will make you feel about ten years old and will give you a terrific workout. It will allow you to display your youthful exuberance and once you've mastered the art again, you'll be able to showcase those hips. To add some extra sizzle, upgrade to a fire hoop!

Talking of sizzle, but of a different sort, I just discovered a rather unusual hobby—collecting **handcuffs**. At first, I thought this might be a tad bizarre but think I can see the logic of it. Imagine the fun you could have locking your husband or children up in handcuffs and then claiming you have lost the key.

4   Source: http://www.fda.gov/fdac/features/1997/297_meno.html
5   http://www.ncbi.nlm.nih.gov/pubmed/22852580

One of the most problematic parts of the menopause for me has been the migraine **headaches**. When you get a bad headache, you can feel awful about almost everything else. Hormonal imbalance during menopause may cause headaches. There are a variety of remedies but before you grab a box of aspirin, think about acupuncture. I admit that at times I would sooner be sticking pins in effigies of people I dislike rather than have someone sticking them in me; however, I should say that acupuncture has helped many women, especially those suffering from migraine headaches.

I also discovered Co-Q-10 thanks to a lovely lady, Chris Tryon, who I met in one of the Facebook menopause groups. It is good for your heart and can also alleviate headaches/migraines. The safest maximum dosage is 100 milligrams twice a day.

If you prefer to ride them out, take heart in the fact that once you are through the menopause, there is a high chance that your headaches will also disappear.

I feel it is my duty at this point, to remind you that sex also helps alleviate those nasty headaches. Research has shown[6] that the release of endorphins from sexual activity can reduce headache pain. It's much more fun than acupuncture and cheaper than a packet of headache pills. So next time you feel a headache coming on, grab your partner and treat them to a workout.

*

I used to get headaches before sex, you know ... "not tonight dear, I have a headache". now I get headaches during sex. my husband whacks me on the head and says, "wake up!"
comedienne kathie dice

*

Do you remember that song by Peter Sellers, Goodness Gracious Me, in which Sophia Loren sings about palpitations? Whenever I get **heart palpitations**, I sing the lyrics of that song to myself. Guess what? It helps calm me down.

---

6   http://www.redorbit.com/news/general/1112798056/sex-cures-headaches-030513/

If you have ever had heart palpitations, you will understand how frightening they can be. You fear the worst and wonder if a heart attack isn't imminent. I usually stick my leg out of bed, since it nearly always happens at night, to get contact with the floor, then sing to myself. Don't sing out loud or your other half will think you are completely mad. Try and sing it with appropriate accents too, for added amusement:

"A flush comes to my face. And my pulse begins to race. It goes boom boody-boom boody-boom boody-boom. Boody-boom boody-boom boody-boom-boom-boom."

I must bring **herbal remedies** to your attention in this section. I have had little personal experience of any herbal remedies, however, I discovered Jan Tucker who is passionate about the uses and benefits of herbs, with good reason, since she has used them to treat a variety of symptoms including bronchitis with great success.

Herbs, and Ayurvedic herbs, also helped her sail through the menopause. Her website is most interesting. Again, I'll leave you to make up your own mind if you want to pursue this. Check her out at http://www.whitelotusliving.com/

As I have mentioned in previous chapters, one of the best ways to deal with all menopausal symptoms, apart from exercising and laughing, is to take up a **hobby**.

There are way too many hobbies to mention in this book but rather than looking at the traditional hobbies that women take up, why not consider attempting an adventurous activity like **hiking, horseback riding, hot rodding, helicopter flying, hang gliding, hockey,** or **hunting?**

*

a man left for work one friday afternoon. instead of going home, he stayed out the entire weekend hunting with the boys and spending all his wages. when he finally got home on sunday night, he was confronted by his very angry wife.

after two hours, she stopped nagging and said: "how would you like it if you didn't see me for two or three days?" he replied: "that would be fine with me." monday went by and he didn't see his wife. tuesday and wednesday came and went with the same results. thursday, the swelling went down just enough for him to see her a little out of the corner of his left eye.

*

There is also the rather unusual activity of **hen racing**. Yes, hen racing. You did read that correctly. Every year, hundreds of hens race against each other down a short course in Bonsall near Matlock, Derbyshire. Owners are not allowed to use anything other than verbal encouragement to help the hens complete the course. So, you get to meet like-minded hen owners, shout your head off and then go home and collect some eggs for tea. Sounds ideal to me.

*

q: who tells chicken jokes?
a: comedihens.

*

There are a few menopausal symptoms that you might experience beginning with the letter H. I have talked about hot flushes and headaches but some women also suffer with **hair loss**. My research suggested that you should have your thyroid checked if you are losing hair, as it might not be due to hormone imbalance and falling levels of oestrogen. Unfortunately, thinning hair or loss of hair can make you feel dreadful about yourself. There are a number of treatments and hair-thickening shampoos available, but often a healthy balanced diet should help.

It is important to have a nutrient-rich diet, so don't embark on any weight loss diet programmes at this time and try not to endure too much stress in your life.

Check out some of my earlier suggestions for laughing and exercising to ease tension and release stress. I found throwing a stress ball at Mr Grumpy worked well for me.

thinGs you shoulD hiDe fROm a woman GoinG thROuGh menopause: iDiots, insensitive RemaRks.

*

Insomnia has been the bane of my life since I began menopause. Many a night has been spent lying awake listening to my other half snore the night away. There is a lot of advice about dealing with insomnia. One of the best ways to get a good night's sleep is to be physically active during the day. You shouldn't perform exercise close to bedtime though, since it might make you more awake.

Avoid large meals, smoking, and working right before bedtime. Don't drink caffeine after noon or alcohol close to bedtime. Try drinking something warm before bedtime, such as caffeine-free tea or warm milk. Keep your bedroom dark, quiet, and cool. Don't watch television or have any other distractions in there. Avoid napping during the day, and try to go to bed and get up at the same times every day. Sprinkle lavender oil on your pillow. If you wake during the night and can't get back to sleep, get up and do something relaxing until you're sleepy.

*

just took some sleepinG pills but they Don't seem to be woR...

*

You name it and I have tried it. None of the above worked for me. In the end, I gave up. My body clearly doesn't want to sleep, so I may as well use the time productively. I spend nights awake typing my books, posts and articles in the quiet. It seems I am at my most creative during these peaceful hours. The bonus is that about three o'clock in the morning, I get sleepy and grab a couple of good hours' sleep. Better that than a night half awake and frustrated.

I am of the opinion that your body will decide what it needs. About one in every seven nights I conk out completely and enjoy a good rest. That does it for me. I believe that Margaret Thatcher and Winston Churchill survived on only a few hours' sleep each night, so why worry about it?

*

patient: "ꝺoctor, ꝺoctor, i can't get to
sleep."
ꝺoctor: "sit on the eꝺge of the beꝺ anꝺ
you'll soon ꝺrop off."

*

Irritating symptoms of the menopause include **itchy skin, irregular periods, irregular heartbeat** and **irritability**.

Going through the menopause prepares us for the next stage of our lives—becoming a grumpy old woman. Do you get **irritated** by people? I find whereas I used to have bucket loads of patience with everyone nowadays, I get irritated by minor habits, small things and most people for no apparent reason.

Have you noticed that old people have a habit of walking in front of you, no matter which direction you go? They don't seem to be able to walk in straight lines and cut diagonally across in front of you, tripping you up with those shopping trolley bags that they insist on pulling along behind them. Worse still, they can be standing outside a shop staring at the window but the second you attempt to overtake them, they set off at a slow pace and cut right in front of you. My husband says that they are like mini Daleks, all shooting off in various directions blocking your path, oblivious to you behind them. It's terrible if you are in a supermarket and they are steering a supermarket trolley down the aisles. Look out for them. They have no rear view mirrors and those trolleys can really hurt your ankles.

Should you wish to hang out with other grumpy old women and have a jolly good rant about what irritates you, start your very own Grumpy Old Women's Club online forum or blog giving everyone the opportunity to have their say. You will be surprised at how many of us like to have a chunter.

you are becoming a grumpy old woman when instead of tutting at old people who take ages to get off the bus, you tut at rowdy school children.

*

Itchy skin can be most irksome. Some days, I scratch and scratch. For no apparent reason, my skin will become incredibly itchy and before long, I will have raised a red rash. If you have this symptom, then check out websites for advice on what to do. The menopause site http://www.34-menopause-symptoms.com/ recommends that you have an increased intake of omega-3 fatty acids, and an increased water intake. Avoid hot showers or baths, moisturize after showers, use gentle, non-irritating soaps, use a quality, broad-spectrum sunscreen, and avoid other irritants such as smoke, stress and lack of sleep.

After scratching my head for about half an hour the other day, Mr Grumpy offered to buy me a flea collar. I bit his leg.

Irregular periods or heavy periods are common at this time of our lives. Like a good Girl Guide, be prepared. Even when you think that they might have finished completely, they could start up again after a few months without warning. They will stop eventually and you'll not have to fret about being caught out again.

*

pms jokes aren't funny, period.

*

This last symptom of menopause beginning with the letter I is one that embarrasses many of us—**incontinence**, particularly stress incontinence. Yes, that awful moment when you acknowledge the fact that you shouldn't have laughed too much. What can I say about it other than suggest you make lifestyle changes, take up pelvic floor muscle exercises or try out Pilates exercises?

*

SIGNS YOU MAY BE EXPERIENCING the
menopause:
you change your underwear after every
sneeze.

*

One of my friends, who teaches Pilates in France, has been thanked by the local doctor for single-handedly helping local women of a certain age overcome stress incontinence. There is a considerable amount of good advice if you are experiencing stress incontinence, so don't be ashamed. Seek professional advice.

*

advert: pilates of the caribbean
just twenty minutes every day, and your
muscles will be blooming in no time! and
your figure will doubtless take on a whole
new depp!

things you should hide from a woman going through menopause: knives, kinder chocolate, kit kats.

*

Why did I leave out the letter J, you ask? I struggled to find relevant material other than **journal writing** which might help you explore your thoughts and feelings towards yourself and the menopause and **joint ache**, so I jumped over it to the letter K.

There is not a lot to discuss under this letter either, other than to suggest that you might like to take up the hobbies beginning with that letter including **knitting** or **kayaking**. I don't mean knitting socks or anything too ordinary. Have a go at a record like the residents of Bupa care homes who managed a world record tea cosy on 9th April 2009. The final tea cosy included 1924 squares in total. It stands at 3.9 metres high and 11.1 metres on circumference.

You could enjoy two hobbies at once and attempt to knit a scarf while running a marathon. This record is currently held by Susie Hewer from the UK who knitted a 1m 62 cm scarf while competing at the Flora London Marathon on April 13th 2008.[7]

Kayaking can be very soothing when you embark on a gentle trip down a river or you could give yourself a thrill and attempt kayaking down a waterfall. Either way, I suggest you go in a single kayak. The last trip I took in a kayak with Mr Grumpy and friends resulted in us paddling in circles for over half an hour, then bickering for a further half hour until our friends took pity on us and separated us, allowing each of us to sit with one of them. We then turned into competitive fiends and paddled down the river at breakneck speed. It ended badly with my kayak crashing into a large rock at the bottom of a weir, where it overturned and I had to be rescued by some French people who were watching us from their picnic spot by the river.

7   www.guinnessworldrecords.com

Needless to say, Mr Grumpy won the race and was horribly smug for the rest of the day.

*

two eskimos sitting in a kayak were getting cold, so they decided to light a fire in their boat. it promptly sank, proving once again that you can't have your kayak and heat it too.

thinGs you shoulδ hiδe from a woman GoinG through menopause: LonGBows, Lunatics, LiGht saBeRs.

*

Luckily, I could only find one menopausal symptom beginning with the letter L —**loss of libido.** I also discovered a rather amusing video on YouTube. The *"Don't Touch Me Menopause rap song"* from Planetsweetpea.com and based on the MC Hammer hit *"You Can't Touch This"* has attracted over 68,000 hits so there must be a lot of menopausal women who watched it. It's worth a look. Warning—you might find yourself singing it for days on end.

It is possible that hormones, especially lack of oestrogen, are to blame for loss of libido. However, there is evidence that says it is not. However, "Contrary to myth, the menopause doesn't usually cause loss of libido, and indeed many women feel a lot sexier and have more orgasms in the postmenopausal part of their life."[8]

Armed with that information, I suggest you nip down to your local sex underwear store and stock up on goodies.

If you do suffer from loss of libido, seek advice. It might be due to other factors. (My eighty-year-old mother suggested that if I suffered from lack of sexual desire, I should swap Mr Grumpy and get a toy boy, but I am almost certain she was just joking.)

*

"makinG Love useδ to make my toes cuRL, now it Gives me foot cRamps." comeδienne kathie δice

*

---

8   http://www.netdoctor.co.uk/sex_relationships/facts/lackingsexdrive. htm#ixzz2OGZKuUvt

If, thanks to the menopause, you feel sexier and have an urgent desire to leap on top of your man every night, then **learn a language**. You could seduce him in a foreign language, such as French. Learning a language is excellent for helping your memory too. That's useful. At least you'll be able to remember your man's name when you cry out in ecstasy.

Because it begins with the letter L, I would like to look briefly at **lemongrass** which can be of benefit to some women during the menopause and is mentioned on many websites. Thanks to its ability to energize, it can be used for fatigue and jet lag. In Indian medicine it is used to reduce infections and fevers. As with everything, what works for some individuals may not work for others.

Laughter is one of the most powerful "tools" you possess. A good giggle can help you through the menopause. Humour therapy (sometimes called therapeutic humour) uses the power of smiles and laughter to aid healing. Humour therapy helps you find ways to make yourself (or others) smile and laugh more. Because it is inexpensive, risk-free, and readily available, there is little reason not to try practicing humour therapy.

I attended one of the many humour therapy classes that are very popular these days. We all shuffled in nervously and were greeted by a vociferous, enthusiastic host who encouraged us all to lie down in a circle so we were touching each other with either our heads or feet. He started off the session with a raucous belly-laugh. We were to follow with our own attempts. Before long, we were all genuinely laughing and tears streamed down our faces as we erupted into gales of laughter. I have never felt so healthy. My muscles felt as if I had had a jolly fine workout and I was in excellent spirits.

Laughing is found to lower blood pressure, reduce stress hormones, increase muscle flexion, and boost immune function by raising levels of infection-fighting T-cells, disease-fighting proteins called Gamma-interferon and B-cells, which produce disease-destroying antibodies. Laughter also triggers the release of endorphins, the body's natural painkillers, and produces a general sense of well-being. Even faking a laugh can fool the body into releasing endorphins, so have a snigger at some silly jokes, even if you don't find them funny. You'll still experience the benefits of laughter.

There is no doubt that laughter can help you when you feel depressed and can lift your mood. Let's give you a quick health check-up:

*

a man went to the doctors because he hadn't been feeling well. the doctor examined him, left the room and came back with three different kinds of pills. "take the red pill with a big glass of water when you get up," the doctor said, "and the yellow pill with a big glass of water after lunch, and the green pill with a big glass of water before you go to bed."

the man looked worried and asked, "but doctor, what's actually wrong with me?" the doctor replied, "you're not drinking enough water."

*

Feeling a little more light-hearted? Good. Time to move on to the letter M.

things you should hide from a woman going
through menopause: machete, mace, men.

a couple is lying in bed. the man says, "I
am going to make you the happiest woman
in the world."
the woman replies, "I'll miss you ... "

*

Mardy, miserable, merry, mad, or all of the aforementioned? Yes, we have all experienced the joys of **mood swings**. One minute you are whistling in the kitchen waiting for the kettle to boil, and the next minute you are slamming drawers shut and grumping about the place. If it weren't so depressing, it would be funny.

Being the sort of Tigger-like character it came as a big shock to suddenly find my thoughts had all turned into morbid ones and I had transformed into an Eeyore. Mood swings are all part and parcel of hormonal changes and as I have mentioned a few times already, a healthy outlook will definitely help you.

Put some cheerful music on, even if you feel like punching the DJ on the radio station for sounding so chipper and perky. Remind yourself that this mood will pass and make an effort to change it. Okay, that is easier said than done, but going out for a quick walk, even on a freezing cold day, with some music on an iPod will improve that mood much quicker than stomping about the house snarling at everyone. Have a go.

*

my husband, being unhappy with my mood
swings, bought me a mood ring the other
day so he would be able to monitor my
moods.

we've discovered that when i'm in a good mood, it turns green and when i'm in a bad mood, it leaves a big red mark on his forehead.
next time, he'll think twice and buy me a diamond.

*

Here is some practical advice for helping with mood swings[9]:
- Get enough sleep and stay physically active. This will help you feel your best.
- Avoid taking on too many duties. Look for positive ways to ease your stress.
- Talk to your doctor. He or she can look for signs of depression, which is a serious illness that needs treatment. You could also consider seeing a therapist to talk about your problems.
- Try a support group for women who are going through the same things as you.
- If you are using HRT for hot flushes or another menopause symptom, your mood swings may get better too.

*

signs you are experiencing menopause: you don't know whether to laugh or cry. sometimes you do both.

*

If you feel moody or if you suffer from insomnia, try creating a **moon garden**.

A moon garden is a garden that is planted specifically to be enjoyed at dusk and in the moonlight. Moon gardens typically have flowers and plants that reflect waning light or moonlight well, or smell their best in the evening.

Moon friendly flowers can get lost during the daylight hours, but at night they shine. Moon friendly flowers will be light in colour, normally white, cream or light yellow. These colours will pop out

9   http://womenshealth.gov/menopause/symptom-relief-treatment/

under the light of the moon and will appear to glow in low light. Try adding petunias, lilies, peonies, yucca, or irises. Try and choose a colour that will look good at night with moonlight on it.

There are many flowers that only produce scent at night and these flowers typically have a stronger scent than their day blooming counterparts. Evening primrose, honeysuckle, jasmine, and, of course moonflowers will reward you. Make sure you add some silver-coloured or variegated foliage, like lamb's ears, golden oregano, or hostas.

On a bad night when you can't sleep, go outside to your moon garden and enjoy the delights it has to offer or garden by the luminescent glow of the moon's light. It'll keep you cool, calm, and collected.

My mother and I have had a good old chuckle about the next symptom of menopause—**memory loss**.

*

patient: "doctor, doctor i've lost my memory."
doctor: "when did this happen?"
patient: "when did what happen?"

*

During a phone call, I told her that I had gone to the kitchen and couldn't remember why. I had opened the fridge and found that I had put the washing up liquid in it. She laughed loudly and told me that it was going to get worse, and to prepare for the ride. I listened to her advice. After all, mums know best.

She regaled me with a tale of how she had left her walking stick in the supermarket, hanging from a trolley. She had managed to get all the way back to her car carrying her shopping bags, then spent ages trying to get into her car. The key wouldn't work and she was getting more and more exasperated with it as she tried to wiggle it in the lock. Several minutes later, having peered at her key and fumbled about she looked inside the car. It wasn't her car. It wasn't even the same make as her car, only the same colour.

Once she'd finished choking with laughter about it, she found her car and loaded her shopping in. She still forgot to go back and look for her walking stick though.

Memory loss can be quite frightening; however, I read a study that assured me that memory loss due to the menopause is only temporary. If you think you are experiencing some memory loss then games and little puzzles are just what you need.

*

SIGNS YOU ARE EXPERIENCING MENOPAUSE: YOU HAVE TO WRITE POST-IT NOTES WITH YOUR KIDS' NAMES ON THEM.

*

Tightness in the muscles, especially back, shoulder, neck and abdomen. Tension headaches. Fatigue. Muscle tenderness, muscle spasm, and muscle pain. "These are a few of my least favourite things … " Sorry, I just had to burst into song there. As women approach menopause, many will notice the onset of **muscle tension**. This is a common menopausal symptom that is a normal part of getting older; however, there are treatments that can help alleviate muscle tension related to menopause.

There are a variety of ways to treat muscle tension through the use of stress relief techniques. These can include deep breathing exercises, meditation, massage and yoga. Exercise can also help relieve muscle tension because it strengthens the muscles as well as relieves stress.

Tai Chi is an ancient **martial art** form that can be extremely beneficial for sufferers of chronic pain and muscle tension. Because it combines both physical and mental relaxation techniques, Tai Chi is an excellent way to treat muscle tension because this menopause symptom results from both physical and mental problems.

You could always resort to getting massages from your beloved to help when tension strikes. Naturally, he'll prefer you to give him a massage before returning the favour but you may be lucky so it won't hurt to ask.

things you should hide from a woman going through menopause: nothing.

*

Night sweats, the nocturnal cousin of hot flushes, are one of the most common companions of menopause. Scientific studies suggest that as many as seventy-five per cent of menopausal women experience night sweats.

One study found that approximately nineteen per cent of women aged forty to fifty-five who still had regular periods experienced night sweats. Most women begin to develop symptoms three to ten years before actual menopause. Research also shows that not all women are affected the same. Age, race, and other factors can influence how likely a woman is to develop night sweats during menopause.

Fortunately, many women have found simple lifestyle changes can provide swift, lasting relief. Preventing night sweats can be achieved with methods such as avoiding overheated bedrooms and reducing stress levels. Dietary changes such as avoiding spicy foods, caffeine, and hot drinks can also be effective.

Alternative ideas include taking a hot water bottle filled with icy cold water to bed. Earthclinic.com suggests drinking two tablespoons of apple vinegar right before you go to bed. Some physicians recommend that menopausal women take magnesium supplements to lessen night sweats.

On a personal note, I couldn't find a relief from them. I should point out here that I'm a person who loves heat. I am a fire sign. I relish feeling the sun on my face and back. I burrow under thick duvets in summer, ensuring my head is completely covered. My husband complains all the time about my freezing cold feet which I warm by sticking them on his toasty warm body. I would happily sit on a Caribbean beach in summer at midday (under a parasol, naturally) but when night sweats occurred, not even throwing off bed clothes and hugging a cold pack from the freezer helped me. The best I could do was laugh about it.

There are a few reasons as to why you could experience **nausea** during menopause and one of those is tiredness. Nausea is likely to pass and, as we have discovered several times already in this book, simple life changes, exercise and healthy diets can assist.

things you should hide from a woman going through menopause: peashooters, pistols, pickaxe, pikes, pepper-spray.

*

One of the most frightening experiences I had was my first **panic attack**, also referred to as panic disorder. I believed I was going to die from a heart attack. Because of the hormonal fluctuations occurring inside the menopausal woman's bodies, several physical and psychological effects take place, and panic disorder may be one of them.

Panic attacks are characterized by unexpected and repeated episodes of intense fear accompanied by physical symptoms that may include chest pain, heart palpitations, and shortness of breath, dizziness, or abdominal distress. These episodes are referred to as panic attacks and may resemble a heart attack.

Once I learned what was happening, I was prepared for the next attack and dealt with it much better. After a few more attacks, I could control them. They nearly always occurred at night, and I found making contact with the floor or a bedside cabinet would help. (Except when I made connection with the bedside cabinet using my head.) Deep breathing and reminding yourself that it is not dangerous will help.

Anyway, let's move away from the possible symptoms of the menopause by introducing **positive thoughts**.

Lauren Bacall once said; "I am not a has-been, I'm a will-be." We should feel that way too.

Positive thoughts will certainly assist you during this time. Researching for this book allowed me to discover many inspirational women whose attitude about ageing is to be admired and emulated.

You only need to open a magazine or read a newspaper to be inspired by women of our age: Lulu, Madonna, Michelle Pfieffer,

Kim Basinger, Jane Seymour, Twiggy, Debbie Harry ... the list goes on and on.

You should not feel that you have reached the end of your useful time or indeed your looks, even though there are days when you will inevitably feel demoralised. Ensure you look after yourself, then do or wear whatever you please. Take heart from the example of Dame Helen Mirren who hit the headlines when she sported a red bikini and revealed a figure that has to be applauded.

Looking at any one of a growing number of confident successful women who are enjoying radiant health and opportunities in their fifties and sixties, you cannot feel other than encouraged. Jamie Lee Curtis, who is a long-running actress and best-selling author, is a shining example of what you can accomplish when you love your body the way it is. She posed topless and did a piece on herself called Top Thighs to expose her imperfect body as a spoof on her figure during the filming of Top Lies.

Newspapers, magazines, and the internet are filled with stories from strong women who have transformed their lives following the menopause. There is an abundance of material and a whole host of websites to lift your spirits. In brief, there is little reason for you to feel too dispirited about the menopause. Embrace your body. Learn to love yourself and you'll sail through the next few years with purpose.

There is further good news that once you have got through the menopause, periods will be a thing of the past and you'll be able to wear white trousers once more. You won't get hormonal headaches, monthly mood swings, or PMT symptoms. You'll be able to enjoy sex without worrying about pregnancy and you'll be able to maintain regular cycles of energy with much less fatigue.

*

two hydrogen atoms walk into a bar.
one says, "i've lost my electron."
"are you sure?"
the first replies, "yes, i'm positive ... "

*

So what should you do with all that new energy? Take up pole dancing? That's exactly what grandmother Sun Fengqin of Nanjing, China did. She decided to try the activity after watching several videos and having become fascinated by the beauty and athleticism of pole dancing. She soon became an internet sensation herself and if you Google her you'll discover not only how youthful Sun is but what a fabulous activity this is.

*

I saw a sheep pole dancing the other day. In a kebab shop.

*

You need to possess a certain amount of flexibility to take up pole dancing, so alternative pastimes or activities that do not require so much energy and can help calm you include **painting** or **photography**. These are two of the most popular hobbies enjoyed by women. It is easy to see why, when each allows you to lose yourself in colours, nature and tranquillity.

Menopause is regarded by many as the gateway to self-recognition and is a wonderful time to take up challenges like this. It fuels the creative fires. Artist Helen Redman has embraced menopause wholeheartedly. She uses her art and teaching abilities to encourage women to "claim their age as a time of heightened creativity and spiritual growth". Her work serves as a catalyst for others to explore the issues she raises, and for women to communicate their knowledge with one another. You can find out more about her from her website www.birthingthecrone.com. If you have any desire at all to paint or take up photography, this is probably the right time to embark on your new venture.

*

q: what do you get if you cross a painter with a boxer?
a: mohammed dali

q: why was the art dealer in debt?
a: he didn't have any monet

q: what did the artist say to the dentist?
a: matisse hurt

*

You would need to be completely crazy to want to take up **parkour** (or free running) which involves running and hurling yourself off buildings and roofs. Having decided it was a hobby practised by many people and after watching lots of videos of people performing mind-boggling jumps, I couldn't find any evidence of women of our age doing it. However, I discovered a course offering injury-free running for women over forty, and learned about Luci Romberg, a thirty-year-old stuntwoman from Colorado who became the world's top female parkour runner in 2012.

I suppose it is a little late in our lives for us to go leaping about and launching ourselves off high buildings. After all, concrete hurts and thanks to a drop in oestrogen, we probably have brittle bones.

Parkour, then, is a no-no, so maybe you could consider taking up a nice soothing hobby like **piano playing**. Once you get past bashing out Chopsticks and daily scales, you'll be able to relax your mind playing beautiful tunes. It's very therapeutic. You'll need patience though. I'm still struggling with Frère Jacques and I think I might be annoying members of my family judging by the earplugs they insist on wearing.

*

a note left for a pianist from his wife:
"gone chopin, (have liszt), bach in a
minuet."

R

thinGs you should hide from a woman going through menopause: Rake, Rubber mallet, Revolver, Rifle, Rapier, Rocket, Rocket launcher.

*

You'll be pleased to learn that I couldn't find any menopausal symptoms beginning with the letter R. Phew!

Following my ridiculous suggestion of parkour in the preceding chapter, let me give you a more sensible suggestion—**running**. Running has obvious benefits for women of all ages and is an ideal hobby to tire you out, improve your stamina, and offer huge health benefits.

A study conducted by Runner's World and the Melpomene Institute looked at more than six hundred women who were both pre- and post-menopausal, at an average age of fifty. Most of these women complained of experiencing a slower pace and increased aches while running—but the number one benefit reported by the women in the study was a relief of the emotional symptoms of menopause. Nearly thirty-one per cent of those in the study referred to the improvement in "emotional health" as being the biggest benefit running brought to their lives.[10]

Women lose up to ninety per cent of their oestrogen in menopause—which causes bone mass to drop two to five per cent annually for the five years following menopause. This increases the risk of osteoporosis, which running unfortunately can't prevent.

According to exercise scientist Steven Hawkins, PhD, "The influence of menopause is beyond what running can overcome," and he strongly recommends strength training for menopausal women as a supplement to their running. "But," says Hawkins, "Osteoporosis is not exclusively about the quality of bone; it's also about the quality of muscle surrounding the bone. If your muscles are built up, you're less likely to fall and break a bone, no matter what state it's in."

10   http://www.runnersworld.com/running-tips/running-your-best-your-50s

A separate study published in the Journal of American Health found that bone density was five per cent higher for women runners in menopause than it was for their "couch potato" counterparts. Furthermore, the journal also reported that women over the age of fifty who did not exercise at least twice a week were eighty-five per cent more likely to develop a bone fracture than their active counterparts. Separately, a Cal-Berkeley study showed that the risk of developing heart disease was decreased for women runners by thirty per cent.

With physical benefits like that, we should seriously consider taking it up. If you need any further encouragement, look to the example of Gladys Burrill, who became the world's oldest female marathon runner at the age of ninety-two. She was a multi-engine pilot, mountain climber, desert hiker and horseback rider but didn't run her first marathon until she was eighty-six years old. There is not much excuse to ignore this hobby, is there? Where did I put my high visibility jacket and old Reeboks?

*

q: what do you get when you run in front of a car?
a: tired

q: what do you get when you run behind a car?
a: exhausted

*

Do you remember the 1970s iconic advert for Nimble bread with a girl, Emily, floating in a hot air balloon to *She Flies Like a Bird* by Honeybus? Try it yourself. You don't need a loaf of bread though. **Riding** in a hot air balloon is less arduous than running and gives you a feeling of exhilaration combined with a sense of calm. If you enjoy this activity, you can consider studying for your hot air balloon licence and you'll feel more able to deal with life's stresses.

Other types of riding that will encourage adrenaline and endorphins to course through you include horse riding and motor bike riding.

"male menopause is a lot more fun than female menopause. with female menopause, you gain weight and get hot flashes. male menopause—you get to date young girls and drive motorcycles."

rita rudner

S

things you should hide from a woman
going through menopause: submachine gun,
saber, shotgun, sickle, saw, switchblade,
slingshot, spiked mace, spear, stun gun.

the seven dwarves of menopause: itchy,
bitchy, sweaty, sleepy, bloated, forgetful
and psycho.

*

One symptom we may suffer from during menopause is thin or
saggy skin. The sun, smoking, alcohol, soft drinks (high in sodium)
can deplete the body's water which affects your skin among other
things.

*

sagging can be prevented. just keep eating
until the wrinkles fill out.

*

There is an abundance of products available that claim to help
with wrinkles and I shall leave you to decide which ones you want to
try out. Creams that contain Retinoid Alpha Hydroxy seem to offer
good results, although new studies are always being offered. Fresh
vegetables and a good diet should also help. If you are inclined, then
botox or fillers are possibilities when fighting the ravages of time,
but I prefer my method of reducing the appearance of wrinkles. It
is cheap, effective and no needles are required. I remove my glasses.
Hey presto! I look immediately younger.

*

a couple on a tight budget were shopping at a supermarket. the husband picked up a pack of twenty cans of beer on offer. "put those back," says his wife, "they cost ten pounds!"
he obeys reluctantly. after choosing some food and milk, the wife stops in front of a display of face creams and slips a pot into the basket.
"hang on, that pot of cream costs twenty pounds," the husband complains.
"but it makes me look beautiful," replies the wife.
"so do twenty cans of beer and they are half the price."

*

In order to take your mind away from sagging skin, you might like to consider some of the following options: **shiatsu, skiing, sewing, swimming** or **stand-up comedy**. Apparently, self-assuredness and quick wit are sexy even if your jokes aren't funny. (Just as well, as most of my jokes are heckle-inducing.)

Be adventurous and go on a **safari**. Think you are wild? Go see some really wild animals.

Try **shooting**. This is a hobby with a certain appeal. You'll create a fine picture with your rifle on your shoulder and a determined expression on your face. There'll be a few folk quaking with fear as you approach. If you really don't want to kill little furry animals, take up clay pigeon shooting. It is just as satisfying. Join any one of a number of shooting clubs all over the country and try small bore, rifle, or air rifle.

Take the plunge and have a go at **scuba diving**. You don't even need to be a good swimmer to become a diver and those rubber suits look good on anyone! I took my PADI licence in a quarry in the UK where it was freezing cold in the murky depths. However, it prepared me for the wonders that I was lucky enough to see later in life while on holiday. The sensation of floating about in clear seas observing multi-coloured fish is one that will immediately make you feel good about life again.

Scuba diving pales into insignificance when you consider the next option to get your pulse racing and your mind cleared of anxieties— **skydiving**. Not for the feint-hearted but being taken up by people of all ages, skydiving is an increasingly popular challenge for many.

Follow the example of Beulah Lewis who, along with three other generations in her family, celebrated a relative's twentieth birthday in 2008 by jumping out of an airplane and skydiving. That might not seem that odd, except Beulah was ninety-eight-years-old at the time.[11]

Or, what about a nice relaxing **spa day**? Have some time out for you and enjoy a day being pampered. Guaranteed to make you purr like a kitten instead of roaring like an angry tigress.

*

I'll spa you the jokes here.

*

Because osteoporosis risk skyrockets following menopause (oestrogen is needed to help lay down bone), **strength training** is important. Try to incorporate at least two weekly strength training sessions to build bone and muscle strength, burn body fat, and rev your metabolism. If you are at home, opt for dumbbells or resistance tubing. If you are a member of the gym, choose from weight machines or free weights.

A woman's risk of numerous medical conditions, including breast cancer, type 2 diabetes, and heart disease rises during and after menopause. Regular workouts and maintaining a healthy weight can help offset these risks, so **stay motivated.**

Swimming is recognised for its health benefits and is enjoyed by many women. So, if you don't fancy being a gym bunny, grab

---
11   Fox News, June 25th 2008

your "cozzie" and head off to the local swimming pool. Pretend you are a member of the cast from Baywatch as you saunter in and dive effortlessly into the waters. Imagination is such a powerful thing.

For those brazen hussies among you, live a little and go skinny-dipping. Not recommended at your local swimming baths.

*

q: In which direction does a chicken swim?
a: cluck-wise.

things you should hide from a woman going through menopause: teargas, tanks, tomahawk, truncheon, tripwire, torpedo.

*

Once again I could find no menopausal symptoms beginning with the letter T so let me talk briefly about the **thyroid**. Many of the symptoms that you experience during menopause such as fatigue, sleep disorders, loss of libido and so on, might be caused by the thyroid and not menopause. If you are at all concerned, go and see your doctor as a simple blood test will determine if your thyroid function is in order.

I stumbled upon **tibolone** and mistaking it for a famous triangular chocolate bar with hazelnuts and honey, I clicked on to discover that tibolone is a hormone treatment taken for symptoms of the menopause such as hot flushes and low sex drive. It can also help prevent your bones thinning. Made in a laboratory, it is supposed to affect your body in the same way that some of your natural sex hormones do. Women taking tibolone were discovered to have:

• Almost half as many hot flushes
• Less sweating
• Less vaginal dryness
• Improved sexual satisfaction
• More sexual fantasies and more sexual arousal
• More desire for sex

If you are interested in this, then check it out[12] and talk to a professional about it. As for me ... I am off shopping for a certain triangular bar of chocolate.

---

12   http://www.webmd.boots.com/menopause/menopause-tibolone

In an effort to tempt you to take up some new activities, I've gathered together a few beginning with the letter T. Terrify your loved ones by taking up **track driving**. There are circuits all over the country where you can leap into a performance car and drive it speedily around a track. You'll be given a lesson on the rules of the circuit and driving safely. Then you'll be put in a car with an instructor who will show you how to line up for apexes and squeeze past testosterone-fuelled men on bends and you'll be able to experience the thrill of racing around a track.

My instructor told me that women are better track drivers because they listen to and act on instructions. At least I think that's what he said in between the screams.

*

q: what kind of car does a shepherd drive?
a: a lamb-orghini.

*

Since watching James Bond in *Live and Let Die* (again) last month, I have developed an interest in **tarot card reading**. (I think part of me imagines I could look like Solitaire from the film if I wear a serene expression and wave a few tarot cards about.)

The tarot is a deck of seventy-eight picture cards that has been used for centuries to reveal hidden truths. In the past few years, interest in the tarot has grown tremendously. More and more people are seeking ways to blend inner and outer realities so they can live their lives more creatively. They have discovered in the tarot a powerful tool for personal growth and insight.

It is believed that the tarot can help you understand yourself better and teach you how to tap your inner resources more confidently. You don't need any "psychic powers" to use the tarot successfully; just develop your natural intuition.

I suppose it comes as no surprise to you to learn that the first card I pulled from the pack was "The Fool".

For those of you who would like to bond with other women and have a rip-roaring good time while working out, join a **tribal belly-dancing** group. American tribal style belly-dancing is a modern take on belly-dancing (see chapter headed B) yet focusses on group improvisation. You often see tribal belly dancers at community events such as festivals and parades. Tribal dancers generally wear wide-legged pants gathered at the ankles (aka pantaloons), tops called cholis and full skirts.

Given that the locals in your home area might not be ready for you dancing outside the village hall, seek out any one of a number of classes in the UK. Look for *FatChanceBellyDance*® studios or sister studios for classes.

I was most intrigued because American style tribal belly dancers not only get to strut their stuff, but they use finger symbols or zils. These are used during fast movement" and there are various patterns you can play using right and left hands. I'm itching to have a go at this.

Great for fitness, lifting the mood and getting you out of the house. Take cover as I shimmy past you singing *Hips Don't Lie* à la Shakira.

*

q: what do you call a belly dancer with a sword?
a: a veiled threat.

*

Perfect your new hobby of tribal belly dancing in Morocco or Egypt with my next suggestion. Go **travelling**—my favourite activity of all. I understand that you might not have stacks of cash to go travelling but I am spending my children's inheritance and taking off whenever possible.

There are endless possibilities and destinations to tantalise you. Travelling does far more than just broaden the mind; it makes you appreciate life and gets you out of a rut. It rejuvenates and settles those chaotic brainwaves.

I have friends who, having journeyed through the menopause, have decided not only to travel, but to make radical changes to their lives and emigrate. There is no doubt that you are likely to want to spread your wings since you have reached this stage in your life.

One friend decided to take up the challenge of becoming a

sommelier and headed off to Italy to study. She now assists people in buying wine. Another friend went off to Australia where she has learned to enjoy outdoor sporting activities and has an all year round tan. She looks about ten years younger. Yet another moved to Canada, learned to drive an eighteen-wheeled truck and wrote all about her adventures.

Those who don't want to leave their homeland might prefer challenges like walking Machu Picchu, paragliding down snow-covered Austrian mountains or running a marathon around the North Pole. The world is a beautiful big place; seize those opportunities while you can.

If money is very restricted, grab a few days away by the sea or in the Peak District enjoying the scenery. Or, consider a house swap with someone from another country. There are websites and organisations that can help you with this.

My last suggestion will help your memory, allow you to mingle with others and stimulate you—**take a course.**

You no longer need to trundle along to an evening class at a college. Courses are springing in schools and education centres at all times of the day and evening. You can do online courses, courses by correspondence or join in at your local village hall. (Tribal dancing wasn't available where I live but yoga, exercise, painting, and other classes were.)

You don't have to sign up for a traditional course. Popular classes include languages, photography, yoga, cookery, computer skills, jewellery making, and family history, however, there is a glut of opportunities including: learning Argentine tango, Bachata, bee keeping, car maintenance (women only), chocolate making (oh yes!), floristry, Mandarin, massage, millinery, plumbing, pole dancing, self-defence, special effects make-up, and zumba among many others. Take a peek at http://www.hotcourses.com/ for some truly inspirational ideas.

This may be just the beginning of the "new you."

Things you should hide from a woman going through menopause: Vice grips.

*

Vaginal dryness and bladder infections are both common with menopause; a natural menopause treatment consists of bearberry and Echinacea. The only caution here is that bearberry can produce unwanted side effects if taken in too large a quantity. However, when either of these supplements are taken properly, it is claimed they do provide significant relief.

*

when you get a bladder infection, urine trouble.

*

Away from the miseries that accompany the menopause and onto ways to combat the symptoms. Have a go at **vigorous housework**. Half-hearted dusting doesn't exactly count. Vigorous housework— the type that elevates your heart rate and utilizes your larger muscle groups like quads, glutes, and your core—does count. This form of aerobic activity will serve you well. If you're a beginner (like me), start with ten minutes of light activity, slowly boosting physical intensity as it becomes easier. Cheaper than the gym and your house will shine.

Given that I have an allergy to housework, I much prefer my next suggestion—**vlogging**. Vlogging derived from "video logging," is a fairly new hobby similar to blogging. You pick a theme such as personal details about your life (like a video journal), or the news/politics, or humorous videos on the internet, or logging a particular activity you're working on (like losing weight or building something) and video it. You could even vlog about how to deal with the menopause.

You will need a decent camera in order to make your video bearable to watch, otherwise you'll end up with grainy videos like those I made until I stole my hubby's camera.

Become a film director and producer and make short films, either with friends, or by yourself. You can enter your short film into contests. (I might even see you at the next Cannes Film Festival.)

things you should hide from a woman going
through menopause: whip, wrench or any
weapon.

*

I'll waft over this next subject—**wind**. I brought it up under the
letter g.

*

patient: doctor, doctor, what can you give
me for the wind?
doctor: try this kite.

*

Weight gain, specifically a thickening in your middle, is yet
another sign of changing hormones. While a number of books and
doctors claim that menopause has nothing to do with weight gain
and that weight gain occurs in menopausal women because they're
older and their metabolism is slowing down, other studies indicate
that hormone levels are tied to weight gain and redistribution of fat.

On average, women gain between twelve and fifteen pounds
between the ages of forty-five and fifty-five, the stage in life when
menopause typically occurs.

This extra weight generally does not evenly distribute itself
throughout a woman's body. The weight tends instead to
accumulate around the abdomen, and women often notice the shape
of their bodies slowly lose their hour-glass figure and begin to take
on a rounded shape.

Of course, weight gain might not be due to the menopause and
instead be linked to poor diet, lack of sleep, and stress. Changes in
diet and exercise can help rev up your body's metabolic rate. Also
trying natural alternative supplements may help.

*

Lady to the doctor over the phone:
"doctor, please prescribe me something
immediately to reduce my weight. my
husband has given me a wonderful birthday
present, and I can't get into it."
doctor: "just come over here tomorrow,
and I'll give you a prescription. then
you'll soon be able to wear your
wonderful new dress."
Lady: "who said anything about a dress? I
am talking about a car."

*

Activities that you could take up to help battle weight gain beginning with the letter W include **weight-lifting, wrestling,** and more sensibly, **walking.** Regular walking will do wonders for you and is much easier on the joints than running. Try to walk every day for at least twenty minutes to half an hour and those pounds will soon shift.

Watching birds, word puzzles, word games, wood carving, water polo, and **wine tasting.** There are plenty of choices for you beginning with the letter W.

I'll leave you with another of my favourite activities, guaranteed to help you through this time—**writing.** Whether it be a journal, diary, blog or book, jot down a few paragraphs every day and transport yourself to another world. Tap into that creativity that is waiting to be discovered and let your feelings flow over the pages. Write short stories, poems, or novels. It is one of the most rewarding activities I have discovered.

*

since women go through menopause, do
men go through womenopause?

X

X is for the extra stuff I couldn't find a home for in other chapters. It's a mixture of jokes about ageing to give you a smile.

*

the thing about being a middle-aged woman is that when you go for a mammogram, you realise it's the only time someone's ever going to ask you to appear topless in a film.

the nice thing about being senile is you can hide your own easter eggs.

it's scary when your body starts making the same noises as your coffeemaker.

you know you're getting older when most of the products in your shopping cart contain the words "fast relief."

middle age is when you choose a cereal because of its fibre content, not the free toy.

what about that awkward moment when you can't remember the name of someone who's enthusiastically greeting you ... so you say, "and ... how are you?"

the doctor says i have insomnia. i'm not going to lose any sleep over it.

my day begins backwards. I wake up tired
and go to bed wide awake.

thirty is a nice age for a woman,
especially if she happens to be fifty.

you're safer teasing a grizzly bear than
telling a woman in menopause that she is
moody.

*

As for activities that you might like to take up that begin with the letter X, I could only come up with **x-treme** sports and **xylophone playing**. I enjoy playing the xylophone. I always have a go at the display models when I am passing through the toy department in large stores. I've mastered *Twinkle Twinkle*. I wonder if Gotye need another member to join their group?

thıngs you should hıde from a woman goıng through menopause: youR wallet.

*

Practice a relaxation technique that works for you—be it deep breathing, **yoga** poses, or meditation. Yoga can help alleviate symptoms like hot flushes, irritability, and fatigue, and the poses can also calm your nerves by centring your mind.

There is an abundance of classes and information about yoga so I shan't go into details here. Yoga's sister science Ayurveda offers a holistic approach to health that maintains balance in the body, mind, and emotions through diet and lifestyle.

Fun activities to take up to make you feel youthful include **yo-yos.** The yoyo or yo-yo is considered the second oldest toy in history, the oldest being the doll. Ready for a quick spot of trivia?

In ancient Greece, the toy was made of wood, metal and terra cotta. The Greeks decorated the two halves of the yoyo with pictures of their gods. As a rite of passage into adulthood, Greek children often gave up their toys, and placed them on the family altar to pay homage. Around 1800, the yoyo moved into Europe. The British called the yoyo the "bandalore", "quiz" or "the Prince of Wales" toy. However, yo-yo is a Tagalog word, the native language of the Philippines, and means "come back". In the Philippines, the yo-yo was used as a weapon for over 400 hundred years. Their version was large with sharp edges and studs and attached to thick twenty-foot ropes for flinging at enemies or prey.

Perform tricks such as "Man on the Flying Trapeze" or "Around the World". (Watch out for low ceiling lights. I smashed the glass shade trying to master the latter.) Or, sharpen the edges of the yo-yo and add studs, depending on your mood.

Yo-yos are now one of the hottest toy collectibles and many models have values in the hundreds or even thousands of dollars so when you get bored with it, store it. It might become a valuable heirloom.

*

why δiδ the yo~yo cross the Roaδ? Because it was walking the δog.

*

A *Life on the Ocean Wave* could be just what you need to stimulate you. **Yachting** courses are available throughout the country including some on reservoirs and lakes. You will get fit and could soon learn to skipper your very own yacht. Sell the house and sail off to Monaco for added amusement.

I was tempted to put **yacking** down as a hobby, but I think it comes with the territory of being a woman. We enjoy a good chat. It is good to have friends at this time of your life so make the most of them and get together for a good old chinwag.

What about starting a **yak** farm? Well, maybe have a small zoo with a couple of yaks in it? Yaks are versatile animals and produce milk.

There are yaks in the UK and so I am not being completely crazy here. I don't suggest you go for a wild yak. In their natural habitat, Yaks live above the snow line in winter, in temperatures as low as minus forty degrees centigrade. They walk following in each other's footsteps. They burrow through the snow for food. In the spring, they form larger herds moving onto the grazing pasture lands. They can also live in the tropics at plus forty degrees centigrade. The male wild Yak can grow to over two metres high and is the largest of all the cattle family. If you go this route, get a domestic yak which is smaller. They are very sure-footed.

*

q: what's a yak's favourite alcoholic δrink?
a: cognyak

q: What do you call a yak that wants to take over the world?
a: a megalomaniyak

q: What car does a yak drive?
a: a cadillyak, of course.

*

Y is for **youthful**. No matter what your age, you can maintain a youthful approach through humour and light-heartedness. Look after your health, eat sensibly, exercise regularly, take up some stimulating activities, and you will be forever youthful. After all, *He who laughs, lasts!*

Z

things you should hide from a woman going through menopause: uzi (yes, that's cheating, but can you think of anything beginning with the letter z?

*

Do you prefer to be around people when you work out? Join a group class at the gym. **Zumba** is a popular dance programme that has swept up nearly twelve million devoted fans in the past decade. Incorporating salsa, merengue, and other Latin-inspired music, Zumba works for people of all ages. It's a great dynamic core workout. It works your entire torso section. You'll get stronger with defined abs and back. You can burn five hundred to a thousand calories in one hour. (That's between two and three and a half Mars Bars.) You'll soon gain a positive self-image when you drop those pounds.

Sign me up!

I couldn't leave you without one zany hobby beginning with the letter Z. For all of you who thought I might offer zebra racing or zorbing, you are wrong. I decided to encourage you to attempt— **zip-lining**.

This is an activity that allows you to soar over a canopy of trees or forests suspended only by a wire. Zip line tours are becoming popular holiday activities, found at outdoor adventure camps or upscale resorts. The jungles of Costa Rica, Florida and Nicaragua are popular destinations for zip line enthusiasts.

The Zip at Adrenalin Quarry in South East Cornwall is the UK's longest zip wire. Their website http://www.adrenalinquarry.co.uk/zip-wire-activities-cornwall/ suggests that you "Throw someone you love off a cliff."

Don't tell me you are too old for this sort of thrill. Ninety-seven-year-old Theresa Richards from Chattanooga, Tennessee, soared on the zip line course at Ruby Falls, USA. After making the trip and wearing a souvenir T-shirt she declared, "Oh it was marvellous! I'd do that again!"

She isn't the only lady to have a go at this activity. I discovered several other elderly ladies and gentlemen who were only too happy to embrace the thrill of speeding above the ground. You'll need a head for heights and a lot of nerve but if you do it, you'll be rewarded with a large dose of adrenalin.

Whatever you decide to take up, enjoy it. This should be the time when you take stock of who you are and where you are going next in your life, so tackle it head on and with enthusiasm.

You can find out more about menopause, symptoms and get advice by visiting my website www.grumpyoldmenopause.com

I leave you with one final crumb of comfort. By the end of 2013, there will be fifty million Women of Menopause.[13] See, you don't feel so alone now, do you?

---

13   http://www.fwhc.org/menopause/meno.htm

About The Author

A graduate of the University of Keele in Staffordshire, Carol E Wyer is a former teacher, linguist, and physical trainer.

She spent her early working life in Casablanca, Morocco, where she translated for companies and taught English as a foreign language. She then returned to work in education back in the UK and set up her own language company in the late eighties.

In her forties, Carol retrained to become a personal trainer to assist people, who, like herself, had undergone major surgery.

Having spent the last decade trying out all sorts of new challenges such as kickboxing, diving, and flying helicopters, she is now ensuring her fifties are "fab not drab". She has put her time to good use by learning to paint, attempting to teach herself Russian, and writing a series of novels and articles which take a humorous look at getting older.

Carol lives in rural Staffordshire with her own retired Grumpy. It is little wonder that she is a regular blogger and social networking addict.

Entertaining (and Award-Winning, too!) Novels by Carol E Wyer

Mini Skirts and Laughter Lines

Amanda Wilson can't decide between murder, insanity, or another glass of red wine. Facing fifty and all that it entails is problematic enough. What's the point in minking your eyes when your husband would rather watch Russia Today than admire you strutting in front of the television in only thigh boots and a thong?

Her son has managed to perform yet another magical disappearing act. Could he actually be buried under the mountain of festering washing strewn on his bedroom floor? He'll certainly be buried somewhere when she next gets her hands on him.

At least her mother knows how to enjoy herself. She's partying her twilight years away in Cyprus. Queen of the Twister mat, she now has a toy boy in tow.

Amanda knows she shouldn't have pressed that Send button. The past always catches up with you sooner or later. Still, her colourful past is a welcome relief to her monochrome present—especially when it comes in the shape of provocative Todd Bradshaw, her first true love.

Amanda has a difficult decision to make – one that will require more than a few glasses of Chianti.

Surfing in Stilettos

Amanda Wilson is all geared up for an exciting gap-year, travelling across Europe. She soon finds her plans thwarted when she is abandoned in France with only a cellarful of Chateau Plonk, a large, orange Space Hopper, and Old Ted, the dog, for company.

Fate has intervened to turn Amanda's life on its head. First, Bertie, the camper van, breaks down. Then her dopey son, Tom, who is staying in their house in the UK, is wrecking it, one piece at a time. Next, the jaw-dropping video Skype calls that her irrepressible mother insists on making are, by contrast, making Amanda's humdrum trip even less palatable.

Finally, she discovers that her new-found, French friend, Bibi Chevalier, had engineered a plan to ensure that her philandering husband would never stray again; unfortunately, Amanda is unwittingly drawn into the scheme, becoming a target.

Meanwhile, on a beach in Sydney, a lonely Todd Bradshaw realises that his first true love, Amanda Wilson, is definitely the only woman for him. Can he get back into her good books and hopefully back into her arms with his latest plan? Or will fate intervene yet again and turn everyone's lives upside down?

Just Add Spice

Dawn Ellis needs to escape from her painfully dull existence. Her unemployed husband spends all day complaining about life, moping around, or fixing lawnmowers on her kitchen table. The local writing class proves to be an adequate distraction with its eccentric collection of wannabe authors and, of course, the enigmatic Jason, who soon shows a romantic interest in her.

Dawn pours her inner frustrations into her first novel about the extraordinary exploits of Cinnamon Knight, an avenging angel -- a woman who doesn't believe in following the rules. Cinnamon is ruthless and wanton, inflicting suffering on any man who warrants it. Little does Dawn realise that soon the line between reality and fiction will blur. Her own life will be transformed, and those close to her will pay the price.

How Not To Murder Your Grumpy

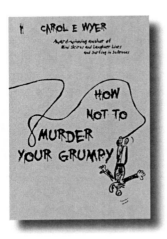

Is your Grumpy Old Man getting under your feet? Is he wrestling with retirement? Are you wondering if you should bundle him up and entrust him to basket-weaving classes? Then this book could be the answer to your prayers. This light hearted guide is packed full of lively ideas, anecdotes and quips. Not only does it set out to provide laughs, but offers over 700 ideas and ways to keep a Grumpy Old Man occupied.

From collecting airline sick bags to zorbing, you will be sure to find an absorbing pastime for your beloved curmudgeon. There are examples of those who have faced extraordinary challenges in older age, fascinating facts to interest a reluctant partner and innovative ideas drizzled, of course, with a large dollop of humour.

Written tongue-in-cheek, this book succeeds in proving that getting older doesn't mean the end of life or having fun. It provides amusing answers to the question, "How on Earth will my husband fill in his time in his retirement?" It offers suggestions on what might, or most certainly might not, amuse him. Ideal for trivia buffs, those approaching retirement, (or just at a loose end) and frustrated women who have an irritable male on their hands, this book will lighten any mood and may even prevent the odd murder.

Lightning Source UK Ltd.
Milton Keynes UK
UKOW04f0001091213

222585UK00005B/120/P